Maths
Outside
and
In

For the Early Years Foundation Stage

Anna Skinner

Acknowledgements

The author would like to thank the staff and children at Ridgeway Primary and Nursery School, Croydon, and in particular

Helen Burns
Yasmin Chaudhry
Joanna Redzimski
Carole Skinner

Thanks also to the following:

Angela Beall, Bardsey Primary School, Leeds
Louise Glover, Bentley Drive JMI School, Walsall
Lynwen Barnsley, Education Effectiveness, Swansea
Andrea Trigg, Felbridge Primary School, West Sussex
Ed Humble, Hampton Wick Infant and Nursery School, Teddington
Emma Kneller, Melody Makers, Gloucestershire
Father Rudolf Loewenstein, St Christina's Primary School, Camden
Elizabeth Wyles, St John's Priory School, Banbury
Kate Joiner, Stroud School, Hampshire
Sharon Sutton, University of Reading
Helen Elis Jones, University of Wales, Bangor
Rachel Richards, Send C of E First School, Surrey
Deborah de Gray, West Kingsdown Cof E Primary School, Kent

The BEAM Development Group:

Joanne Barrett and Tina Rolton, Rotherfield Primary School, Islington
Catherine Horton, St Jude and St Paul's, Islington
Simone de Juan, Prior Weston Primary School, Islington
Sarah Kennedy, Highgate Primary School, Haringey

Published by BEAM Education
Maze Workshops
72a Southgate Road
London N1 3JT

Telephone 020 7684 3323
Fax 020 7684 3334
Email info@beam.co.uk
www.beam.co.uk

ISBN 978 1 9062 2492 9
British Library Cataloguing-in-Publication Data
Data available
Edited by Marion Dill
Design by Reena Kataria
Layout by Reena Kataria and Matt Carr
Illustrations by Vicki Gausden
Printed by Graphycems, Spain

9 8 7 6 5 4 3 2 1

Contents

Introduction

We all know that the best way for children to understand maths is to use their interest and curiosity in the world around them as a springboard. We also know that play underpins learning, and we want our children to be actively involved in a whole range of different experiences to get the most from the environments we create.

The activities in *Maths Outside and In* give children opportunities to play, run, jump, create and manipulate materials, make choices, invent more problems and talk about their solutions. You will find that the suggested activities and experiences build on children's individual enthusiasm and provide a mathematical curriculum that is child led. This type of challenging curriculum is so much richer than one in which children just listen to us adults explaining things. In setting up these experiences, there are possibilities for all children to choose, create, change and be part of a stimulating environment, with lots of opportunities for you and them to be versatile, to experiment and to extend and enhance their learning.

As organisation and space in every early years centre and classroom are unique, I have focused on the two big spaces that everyone has: outside and inside. Focusing on planning for these two spaces together and making connections between the different areas of play opens up a wealth of additional learning opportunities. Outside, children can work on a much bigger scale, make more noise and use larger body movements. There is space for them to use larger tools such as real paint rollers and full-size balls. Inside, there is scope to stimulate experiences and support children's ideas and interests as well as showing them how to use different maths tools and resources.

For both of these two large spaces, outside and inside, I have suggested six themed areas that could be part of your continuous provision or function at different times throughout the year. These are areas where you can organise opportunities to play, provide resources and space, give children time to explore, support them making choices and provide yourself with an opportunity

to observe the children and, most importantly, where you can enhance the maths experiences for all of the children.

Every workshop chapter opens by identifying the maths that the children will experience during play, with an emphasis on problem solving. There are suggestions for additional and specific resources to collect together that will enhance the area: for instance, in the art space there are details of the range of paints and papers that will make it into a very workable workshop area. In addition, there are suggested books and stories to read that reflect the theme as well as music for everyone to listen to and songs to sing along to. You will notice that there are ideas on how to use technology to support maths learning and also what every area needs, which is a maths toolkit of equipment to support the learning.

The individual activity pages for each area identify the maths learning and the vocabulary that you need to use and emphasise. They give good starting points for discussions with the children. I have suggested questions to ask that will encourage children and give them confidence to believe that they can do things themselves or refer them to other children who may be able to help.

Above all, the activities will stimulate and support children's own ideas. Leave time in a discussion for children's reflections and comments, as this will shape your response to the look, listen, note comments that you find with each activity.

What this book provides is lots of ideas, games and activities to enhance and support many different maths learning journeys. You can tailor all the experiences to the needs of individual children, who all deserve first-hand experiences that reflect their interests. I hope you and your children have as much fun and laughter doing the activities as I and the children in my nursery class experienced.

Using the activity pages

You need

This lists the resources you need to provide for the activity.

Words to use

These are words that you use during the activity. Some are everyday words used in a mathematical context. Encourage children to repeat and use the words themselves.

Maths learning

The *Maths learning* section shows you the mathematics covered in each activity. For an in-depth guide, please see the early leaning goals chart at the end of the book.

Mirror dancing

Set up long mirrors in the dance-studio area or line one of the walls with tin foil so that the children can dance to music and watch their reflection as they practise different steps and arm movements. Next, ask children to dance in pairs, with one child being the dancer and the other the reflection of the dancer. The children then change roles. Together, they discuss the differences in the two dances.

You need
- Mirrors or tin foil
- Music of the children's choice

Things to ask

Which steps do you will take your repeat in your dance?
I wonder if you will raise your arms up high in your dance?
How difficult was it to reflect Sam's dance?

Look, listen, note

Which children can:
- create and repeat dance steps to make a pattern?
- discuss the dance routine?
- attempt to reflect another child's action?

Challenge

Children create a pair dance with the same moves. Film the dances. Children then watch and comment on the movements they made.

Words to use

above, below, high, low, in front of, next to, behind, repeat, same, different, opposite

Maths learning

Shape and space
Using everyday words to describe position
Talking about patterns of dance
Showing awareness of symmetry

68   Maths Outside and In

Dance mats

Provide children with dance mats on which to perform a dance that lasts for a minute. Talk about using the whole of the mat for their dance. Children listen to fast and slow dance music for a minute each. Use the one-minute sand timer and make sure that the children understand that both pieces of music lasted for the same amount of time. Children each decide whether they want to dance to fast or slow music. They rehearse their dances on the mats, using lots of different steps, turns and jumps, including lying down.

You need
- Rectangular dance mats or yoga mats
- Fast and slow dance music
- A CD player
- A one-minute sand timer

Things to ask

Does your dance cover the whole length of the mat?
Are you dancing to the fast or the slow music?
What does it mean if your dance finishes before the music stops?

Look, listen, note

Which children can:
- tell on which part of their mat they perform their dance?
- identify whether their dance is fast or slow?
- explain how the sand timer works?

Challenge

Children create a dance to different music.
Children use different-shaped dance mats such as circles.

Words to use

fast, slow, minute, time, timer, turn, forward, back, sideways, pattern, length, width, edge, centre, end, before, after, too short, too long

Maths learning

Shape and space, measures
Using everyday words to describe position
Talking about and creating dance patterns
Using everyday language related to time

Dance studio   69

Main activity

The main activities in *Maths Outside and In* cover a range of mathematical experiences. You can use the activities flexibly to accommodate the requirements of the children in your setting.

Things to ask

Open-ended questions stimulate children's thought processes and encourage the use of mathematical vocabulary. We have given three sample questions for each activity.

Look, listen, note

This section gives you ideas of what to look out for when you assess the children's mathematical understanding as well as their personal and social development.

Challenge

Here, you find suggestions for extending or varying the activity for older or more able children.

Art space

An outdoor art space lends itself to some brilliant experimentation on a large scale. The outdoor art space should differ from one indoors by providing resources that are much bigger in size than you would use inside, such as large sheets or rolls of paper fixed onto railings or walls. Children can use big brushes and rollers or natural objects to create imaginative artwork. Draw children's attention to and compare the sizes, using words such as *large, larger, largest*. Make observations and ask questions such as: "Do you think these brushes are wider or narrower than the brushes we have used before?"

Maths learning chart

Maths content

Activities	Page	Number	Calculating	Shape and space	Measures	Problem solving
Shape shadows	8		☀	☀		☀
Texturing	9			☀	☀	☀
Washing squirts	10			☀		☀
Cylinder collage	11	☀		☀		☀
Snail trails	12			☀	☀	☀
Dry paint	13			☀		☀

Problem solving identified

Activities

Problem solving	Shape shadows	Texturing	Washing squirts	Cylinder collage	Snail trails	Dry paint
Solving problems	☀	☀		☀		☀
Representing			☀			
Decision making	☀	☀		☀	☀	☀
Reasoning		☀				
Communicating	☀	☀	☀	☀	☀	☀

Making the most of your art space

Resourcing the art space

Encourage the group to help collect resources for the art space: large rollers, decorators' paint brushes, wallpaper rolls; small hand brooms to use as paint brushes, window cleaners' rollers, bath sponges.

Developing a learning conversation

Can you tell me about your design?

Why did you decide to use that size brush?

How could you make a textured paint similar to the tree bark?

Using ICT to support maths

Microscope to show pattern detail on natural objects

Digital camera to record artwork

Light box to highlight interestingly shaped objects

Maths toolkit

Rulers, measuring tapes, large 2D and 3D shapes, calculator

Books to read

Rainbow Joe and Me by Maria Diaz Strom (Lee and Low Books Inc)

Who Ever Heard of a Tiger in a Pink Hat? by Nicola Stott McCourt (Meadowside Children's Books)

What Makes a Rainbow? by Betty Schwartz (Piggy Toes Press)

Songs to sing

Lavender's blue, dilly, dilly

Dancing rainbow colours

Music to listen to

Ana Wehabibi by Mahmoud Ahmed

Blue Sky Calling by Lopa

Watermark by Enya

Shape shadows

In this activity, children work in pairs. Together, they choose five shapes each, altogether 10 shapes, some of which will be the same. They share a piece of large, black sugar paper, draw round the shapes with felt-tip pens and cut them out, leaving the sugar paper whole except for the 10 cut-outs. The children each hold an end of their large paper, with the sun behind them, so that the shadows of the shape cut-outs reflect onto a wall or the ground. By holding the paper at different angles, the children can make the shapes change.

You need

- A collection of plastic or wooden shapes
- Large pieces of black sugar paper
- Yellow and pink felt-tip pens
- Scissors

Things to ask

How many more shapes do you need to cut out?

Why did you decide on those shapes?

Which shape shadows do you recognise?

Look, listen, note

Which children can

- count out the shapes?
- use the language of shape in talk?
- select particular named shapes?

Challenge

Children make a zigzag book explaining how to make shape shadows.

Children use the same shape five times to make an individual shape-shadow sheet.

Words to use

how many?, total, altogether, one, two, three ... ten, reflect, reflection, shadow, square, triangle, circle, star, rectangle, hexagon, small, large, corner, side

Maths learning

Calculating, shape and space

Finding the total number of objects in two groups by counting

Using the language of shape

Recognising similarities and differences of shapes

Texturing

To start with, take the children on a walk to collect the natural material they need: small flowers and grasses, dried leaves (to be crumbled up) and twigs. Together, they sort their materials into groups and mix each group with one paint colour to create texture. The texture mixture that works well is half paint, half texture material and a tablespoon of glue. Children use the textured paint with large rollers, brushes and sponge shapes to create designs on lengths of reversed wallpaper.

Things to ask

Can you explain how you sorted your materials?

I wonder what shapes you used to make your design?

What textures did you choose to use?

Look, listen, note

Which children can

- talk about how they sorted out the natural materials?
- talk about their design or pattern?
- identify the different shapes they used?

Challenge

Children decide where to display the wallpaper length when it is dry.

Children identify other materials that would make good textured paints.

Washing squirts

Ask the children to help peg a large sheet on a washing line and put a plastic sheet or newspaper on the ground underneath the sheet to catch paint drips. Fill squeezy bottle with watered-down paint in a range of colours. Invite children to make designs by squirting the paint at the sheet.

Things to ask

Did you squirt any curved or zigzag lines?

Can you see any shapes you have made in your design?

I wonder if there are any parts of your design that look the same?

Look, listen, note

Which children can

- identify any symmetrical parts of their design?
- use shape words to describe parts of their design?
- identify types of lines such as 'curved' or 'straight' on their design?

Challenge

Children write labels to attach to the sheet, identifying shapes and different types of lines.

Children make a large display of their designs.

Words to use

line, straight, curved, zigzag, square, triangle, circle, spiral, pattern

Maths learning

Shape and space

Using the language of shape

Using everyday words to describe position

Showing awareness of symmetry

Cylinder collage

Children work together to make a 3D collage sculpture on a large circle of cardboard, using a variety of cylinders, tubes and paper cups. Draw the children's attention to how they could attach the cylinders at right angles to each other with paper clips or how small cylinders can slot inside another, larger one. Talk about balancing cups on top of one another or lying down end to end. Give children an opportunity to experiment with how the materials can fit together before they begin to assemble their sculpture.

You need

- Cardboard circles to use as sculptures bases
- A large collection of tubes, including empty wrapping-paper rolls, paper-towel tubes, paper cups, sweet tubes, art straws
- Paper clips
- Masking tape, PVA glue
- Paper clips, bulldog clips, plastic connectors

Things to ask

How can you find out which cylinder is the tallest?

Can you describe how you put together your sculpture?

How many cylinders did you use to make your sculpture?

Look, listen, note

Which children can

- select different-sized cylinders?
- discuss how they assembled their sculpture?
- use positional language in talk?

Challenge

Children write a list of contents they used.

Children describe their sculpture, using positional words.

Words to use

solid shape, hollow shape, curved, circle, round, tall, short, wide, narrow, cylinder, next to, position, above, below, in front, count, how many?, altogether

Maths learning

Number, shape and space

Using the language of shape and number

Recognising similarities and differences in size

Using positional language

Snail trails

Children find watching snails move fascinating and will always happily become involved in searching them out. Observing the trails the snails leave as they travel across the black paper is a good stimulus for the children to create their own snail trails, using glue. Provide the children with black paper and glue spreaders so that they can make their own snail trails. When they have drawn the trails with the glue spreaders and before the glue has dried, children sprinkle on white powder paint, using a plastic teaspoon, and shake off any that has not stuck to the paper. Finally, they measure the lengths of their trails.

You need

- A piece of black sugar paper for each child
- Magnifying glasses
- Glue spreaders
- Dry white powder paint
- Plastic teaspoons
- Measuring materials such as string, cubes, sticks, measuring tapes

Things to ask

Can you describe one of your snail trails?

What snail trail do you think is the shortest?

What can we use to measure the trails?

Look, listen, note

Which children can

- describe snail trails using shape words such as 'straight' and 'curved'?
- discuss snail trails using measurement words such as 'longer' and 'shorter'?
- suggest ways of measuring the snail trails?

Challenge

Children draw trails made by other animals or insects.

Invent a snail-trail game, using snails made with malleable materials.

Words to use

line, straight, curved, zigzag, spiral, long, longer, longest, short, shorter, shortest

Maths learning

Shape and space, measures

Using the language of shape

Comparing lengths

Using the language of measurement

Dry paint

Children paint the paper with a sugar solution, making the paper quite wet. They then sprinkle dry powder paint across the paper, using the shakers. The children watch and give a commentary as the colours merge together. They use a cotton bud to draw a pattern of curved lines, swirls and spirals and 2D shapes across the merged paint colours.

You need

- Large pieces of paper
- A thin solution of icing sugar and water
- Large brushes and paint trays
- Dry powder paint in various colours
- Shakers or pepper pots
- Cotton buds

Things to ask

What happened when you sprinkled the paint on your paper?

Can you say how you made your pattern?

Did you draw any shapes in your pattern?

Look, listen, note

Which children can

- make observations on their painting?
- talk about how they constructed their pattern?
- identify shapes in their pattern?

Challenge

Draw a pattern and recreate it, using dry-powder paint techniques.

Write instructions telling others how to do a painting, using dry powder paint.

Words to use

curved, spiral, line, shape, circle, pattern

Maths learning

Shape and space

Talking about and being aware of movement

Creating and describing patterns

Using the language of shape

Caves and dens

Children, particularly boys, love creating caves and dens which become magical places to play in. In order to have ownership of the den and to maximise learning, involve children in their construction, with their ideas leading the way. Encourage children to explore the resources and discuss which materials would be best to use. Point out how important it is to work together when building a den. Offer extra resources as needed and support the children's ideas by cutting or joining boxes or material that they cannot manage. It is better to let children choose where to position their cave or den unless, of course, there is a safety aspect to consider.

Maths learning chart

Maths content

Activities	Page	Number	Calculating	Shape and space	Measures	Problem solving
Outdoor den	16			✵		✵
Superheroes' house	17				✵	✵
The '10' tent	18	✵				✵
Wildlife hide	19	✵	✵			✵
Bear cave	20	✵		✵		✵
Bookspace	21	✵	✵			

Problem solving identified

Activities

Problem solving	Outdoor den	Superheroes' house	The '10' tent	Wildlife hide	Bear cave	Bookspace
Solving problems	✵	✵	✵	✵	✵	✵
Representing			✵		✵	✵
Decision making	✵	✵	✵	✵	✵	✵
Reasoning		✵	✵			✵
Communicating	✵			✵		✵

Making the most of your caves and dens

Resourcing caves and dens

Encourage the group to help collect resources for the caves and dens: tablecloths and curtains, sheets, camouflage netting; props for frames such as table legs; sheets of bubble wrap, plastic shower curtains; tripod joiners, duct tape and gaffer tape; plastic curtain tracks, bulldog clips, safety pins; pulleys and ropes.

Developing a learning conversation

Can anyone think of another idea?

Why are you sure that not everybody will fit in the cave?

Can you tell us how you worked it out?

Using ICT to support maths

Mobile phones

Digital camera

Maths toolkit

Measuring tapes, number cards, weighing balances and scales, 3D shapes

Books to read

We're Going on a Bear Hunt by Michael Rosen and Helen Oxenbury (Walker Books)

You're not so Scary, Sid by Sam Lloyd (Templar Publishing)

Stickman by Julia Donaldson and Axel Scheffler (Alison Green Books)

Everyone Hide from Wibbly Pig by Mick Inkpen (Hodder Children's Books)

Songs to sing

The old woman who lived in a shoe

A mouse lived in a little hole

Music to listen to

The Lark Ascending by Ralph Vaughan Williams

Concerning Hobbits by Howard Shaw

Outdoor den

Children can spend hours exploring large cardboard boxes with friends. In this activity, encourage the children to find out how many of them can get inside a box and whether they prefer an open flap as a door or just an open space. Extend the play by providing a second box and encourage the children to think about joining the two together to make a house. Show them how to cut along two sides of each box to turn them inside out and, together, discuss the best way to join them.

You need

- Two large cardboard boxes
- Cutting tools
- Paint
- Brushes and rollers
- Masking tape

Things to ask

What side will you tape together?

I wonder how many corners there are on these boxes?

What is the best shape to cut out as a window?

Look, listen, note

Which children can

- use the language of shape in talk?
- offer suggestions for window shapes?
- recognise some 2D shapes and 3D solids?

Challenge

Children paint and decorate the outside of the house.

Children furnish the house with cushions and use smaller boxes to make tables.

Words to use

corner, side, square, circle, edge, flat, rectangle, cube, cuboid

Maths learning

Shape and space

Using mathematical terms to describe shapes

Using familiar objects and shapes to build models

Describing solutions to practical problems

Superheroes' house

Using plastic milk crates as large building blocks, children create a building for superheroes. Talk with the children about stability and look at brick patterns to see how to fit the crates together. Show them how building four columns, 'laying the floor' (using the foil blanket) and using card for the roof will make an instant house. Together, discuss what height the building needs to be and provide measuring equipment.

You need

- Plastic milk crates
- A silver foil survival blanket for floor covering
- A piece of card for the roof
- Measuring tapes

Things to ask

How wide does the superheroes' house need to be?

How high will you build the walls?

How many superheroes can sit in the house?

Look, listen, note

Which children can

- talk about the width or the length of the house?
- discuss how high the walls of the house need to be?
- offer a strategy for finding out how many can fit in the house?

Challenge

Children construct a roof for the den so that the superheroes keep warm and dry.

Children extend the house.

Words to use

long, longer, longest, tall, taller, tallest, high, higher, highest, width, length, height

Maths learning

Measures

Using the language of measurement to describe size

Describing solutions to practical problems

Ordering objects by length or height

The '10' tent

Children construct a tent den where everything is counted in tens. To create a '10' tent, count out 10 pegs and peg the material to the line, using sandbags to secure the edges of the material. Together, lay down a rug and label small chairs 1 to 10, using masking tape and card. Children write numbers and pin up a 1–10 number line. Invite the children to use the baskets to make up collections of 10 objects to resource the '10' tent. Children then go on a scavenger hunt to find natural objects to group in tens for the tent. They make a banner identifying the '10' tent.

You need

- A washing line and 10 pegs
- A large piece of material such as two curtains joined together with duct tape
- 10 small bags or football socks filled with sand
- A rug
- 10 small chairs
- Masking tape
- Sticky labels and blank cards to write 1 to 10 for chairs and make a number line
- A collection of natural objects or small-world equipment and baskets
- Banner-making equipment

Things to ask

How can you find out how many pegs there are?

How can we make sure we have the same number of sandbags each side of the tent?

Can you think of a way to find out which number is missing from the number line?

Look, listen, note

Which children can

- count out objects accurately?
- recognise numerals on the number line?
- explain a way of identifying which number chair is missing?

Challenge

Write a rota for checking the number of objects.

Children collect 10 soft toys, give each a number label and sit the toys in the correct number chair.

Words to use

one, two, three … ten, count, count up to, numeral, how many?, how many more?, enough, too many

Maths learning

Number

Saying and using number names in order

Counting reliably to 10 objects

Recognising numerals 1 to 10

Wildlife hide

Children construct a hide so that they can observe birds and other wildlife that visit their outdoor area. They decide on the best place for their hide and use wooden pallets to construct it. Support them in deciding where the entrance to the hide will be and where to put the view window. Children drape the hide in camouflage netting, cover the floor with a waterproof groundsheet and pin up the bird poster and wildlife info sheet. They put out bird food, hang bird cakes from nearby trees and supply water dishes to encourage birds. Discuss how to fill in a tally sheet and use drawn instead of written categories. Encourage the children to keep a tally of how many birds and other animals they see when viewing the wildlife with binoculars. Some children will also notice lions, tigers and bears as well as ladybirds, bees and butterflies.

You need

- 6 wooden pallets (check for any obtruding nails or splinters)
- Camouflage netting (from camping shops)
- A waterproof groundsheet
- A bird poster and a wildlife information sheet
- Bird food, bird cakes and water dishes
- A clipboard and tally sheet
- Binoculars (real and made)

Things to ask

How many birds do you think you will see?

What insects did you see most?

How can you work out how many that is altogether?

Look, listen, note

Which children can

- count the marks they have made on the tally sheet?
- talk about which insects they saw more of?
- suggest a strategy for working out totals?

Challenge

Children design a poster showing birds that come to the hide.

Children keep a weekly 'Birds we have seen' diary.

Words to use

how many?, one, two, three ... ten, total, altogether, count, most, least, more, fewer

Maths learning

Number, calculating

Counting reliably to 10 objects

Using language such as 'more' or 'less' to compare numbers

Finding totals by counting

Bear cave

To make a cave or den for bears, children place a curtain over a table and collect sticks and leaves to cover up the curtain. They use a blanket as floor covering and either use teddies as occupants of the cave or the children act as bears. Discuss with the children the routes the bears might take to visit other areas of the outdoors. They then use the bear footprints to make bear tracks from the cave to other areas.

You need

- A table
- A curtain as a cover for the table
- Sticks and leaves
- A blanket
- Teddy bears (optional)
- Bear footprints cut out from brown paper

Things to ask

Did the bear tracks go past the climbing frame?

How many bear footprints did it take to go from the cave to the water tray?

If the bears went in front of the bike shed, past the frog pond and behind the sand tray, where would they be?

Look, listen, note

Which children can

- count the bear footprints correctly?
- identify the finishing position of the bear tracks?
- talk about the route the bears took round the outdoor area?

Challenge

Children identify the difference in footprints between the shortest route and the longest route.

Children design, measure and make bear masks.

Words to use

count, how many?, in front, behind, next to, past

Maths learning

Number, shape and space

Counting reliably to 10 objects

Using everyday words to describe position

Finding items from positional or directional clues

Bookspace

Children help make a tepee-like tent to use as a quiet reading area. They construct the tent with stout garden canes and plastic cane connectors, then cover the construction with curtain material and attach it to the canes with the bulldog clips. They furnish the tent with blankets and cushions, and they select a small collection of books and put them in a basket to read in the tent. Outside the tent, display two books, two small boxes and some large containers. Discuss with the children voting for the book they like best by putting a counter in the box next to the book.

You need

- Four thick bamboo canes
- Plastic cane connectors (from garden centres)
- Lightweight curtain material
- Bulldog clips
- Blankets and cushions
- A collection of books
- A basket
- Two small boxes
- Large counters

Things to ask

How can we find out which book most children liked best?

Can you explain how you know that that box has fewer counters?

I wonder how many children voted altogether?

Look, listen, note

Which children can

- count the counters successfully?
- talk about which box has more or less counters?
- explain a strategy for finding the total number of counters?

Challenge

Children decide how to record the result of the vote.

Children organise another vote on two different books.

Words to use

how many?, count, more, less, more than, less than, count, one, two, three … ten, total, difference, altogether

Maths learning

Number, calculating

Knowing that numbers identify how many objects are in a set

Using language such as 'more' or 'less' to compare two numbers

Finding total number of items in two groups

Going to the beach

The daily experience of using sand and water provides a rich context for learning maths. Outdoor sand and water areas are more exciting if they do not just replicate the indoor sand and water activities. The sand needs to be deep and cover as big an area as possible so that real digging, hole making and finding treasure can go on. Outdoor water activities should allow for drainpipes, hoses and floating craft. Water provision is best if you can paddle barefoot, so try to provide at least a paddling pool which you can disguise as an ocean and the sand as a beach. A beach will extend play provision and provide a backdrop for some meaningful maths experiences.

Maths learning chart

Maths content

Activities	Page	Number	Calculating	Shape and space	Measures	Problem solving
Pebble lines	24	☀				☀
Collecting shells	25		☀	☀		☀
Hose patterns	26			☀		☀
Building up	27	☀			☀	☀
Rock pools	28			☀	☀	☀
Fishing	29		☀			☀

Problem solving identified

Activities

Problem solving	Pebble lines	Collecting shells	Hose patterns	Building up	Rock pools	Fishing
Solving problems				☀	☀	
Representing	☀		☀	☀		
Decision making		☀			☀	☀
Reasoning		☀			☀	
Communicating			☀		☀	☀

Making the most of your beach

Resourcing the beach

Encourage the group to collect beach equipment: buckets in different shapes, a range of different-sized spades, rakes; large pebbles, driftwood, shells; small flags; a beach umbrella; towels.

Developing a learning conversation

I wonder how we could find out how many spadefuls of sand will fit in the box?

What do you think we should try?

How did you tackle that?

Using ICT to support maths

Colour Magic Beach Scene

Electronic measure

Solar-light water fountains

Maths toolkit

Measuring tapes, metre sticks, measuring containers

Books to read

Sharing a Shell by Julia Donaldson (Macmillan Children's Books)

Mr Gumpy's Outing by John Burningham (Red Fox)

From Snowflakes to Sandcastles by Annie Owen (Frances Lincoln)

Songs to sing

She sells sea shells on the seashore

I do love to be beside the seaside

Row, row, row your boat

Music to listen to

Fingal's Cave from the Hebrides Overture by Felix Mendelssohn

We're All Going on a Summer Holiday by Cliff Richard

Ya Oud by Amal Murkus

Pebble lines

Children make marks on large pebbles to create their own 1–6 pebble line. Suggest to the children that they choose 6 large pebbles each and write a number on each of their pebbles. They then play games such as putting their pebble numbers in order, turning one pebble over and asking one another to guess the turned-over pebble number. Or they count out some small-world figures and balance the right number on each pebble. They can also throw a dice and collect that many small-world figures to balance on each number.

You need

- A collection of large pebbles (from a garden centre or the beach)
- Different-coloured felt-tip pens
- Large 1–6 dice
- 1–10 number line as a reference
- Small-world figures

Things to ask

I wonder what number you will write next?

How did you guess that the pebble turned was number 4?

How do you know your pebbles are in the same order as Liam's?

Look, listen, note

Which children can

- say some number sequences?
- write some numerals?
- put numbers in order?

Challenge

Children roll a 1–6 dice and turn over all their pebbles in as few rolls as possible.

Children use more pebbles to extend their number line.

Words to use

number, one two, three, four, five, numeral, count, the next number

Maths learning

Number

Using number names

Recognising numerals

Saying and using number names in order

Collecting shells

Scatter some shells and bury others in the sand. Give the children a bucket each and ask them to collect shells by digging or sifting the sand. When they have each gathered some shells, they examine them, using magnifying glasses, describe them and then sort the shells into different sets.

You need

- A collection of different shells
- Collecting buckets
- Small spades and sieves
- Magnifying glasses
- Set rings or plastic plates

Things to ask

I wonder if you collected more than 5 shells?

Can you explain what is the same about this group of shells?

If I gave you this shell, what group would you put it in?

Look, listen, note

Which children can

- count their shell collection?
- use a sorting criterion for their shells?
- compare the number of objects in each set?

Challenge

Children re-sort the shells using other criteria.

Children draw property labels for each set.

Words to use

how many?, more than, less than, altogether, the same as, round, curved, pointed, sharp, spiral, small, large

Maths learning

Calculating, shape and space

Comparing two groups of objects

Using language such as 'more' or 'less'

Sorting objects to identify similarities and differences

Hose patterns

You will need to connect a hose to an outside tap or from an inside sink. Connect a showerhead onto the other end of the hose. Invite the children to make marks, patterns and trails on the ground, using the water hose. Encourage them to make large arm movements and to create swirling spiral patterns. Children could also make patterns by using small watering cans containing watered-down paint and shower the paint onto paper to keep as a record of what they did.

You need

- A hose pipe attached to a water supply and showerhead
- A hard surface or large sheets of paper
- Small watering cans
- Watered-down paint

Things to ask

What can you say about the water pattern you have created?

Can you make some curved or zigzag lines?

How could you draw a circle?

Look, listen, note

Which children can

- use the language of shape?
- describe the water patterns they created?
- comment on the sameness and differences they see?

Challenge

Children use a very small watering can and create similar patterns.

Change the hose head so that children can create different patterns.

Words to use

large, small, rectangle, square, circle, straight, curved, zigzag, spiral

Maths learning

Shape and space

Using the language of shape

Talking about simple patterns

Showing awareness of symmetry

Building up

Scatter a range of small objects across the sand, such as small stones and smooth pebbles, shells and driftwood, and involve children in a scavenger hunt. They collect different objects from the sand and see how many of these they can balance on top of one another to build a tower. After they have built their tower, they take a photograph to record their construction and measure its height.

Things to ask

What do you think is the best object to be the base of your tower?

Why did you balance the shell on the top of your tower?

How can you find out which tower is the tallest?

Look, listen, note

Which children can

- use the language of measurement?
- count how many objects were used?
- order two or three towers by height?

Challenge

Children use a measuring tape to decide the height of their tower.

Children record what objects were used to build their tower and display this next to the photograph of the tower.

Words to use

how many?, one, two, three … ten, tall, taller, tallest, short, shorter, shortest

Maths learning

Number, measures

Using language such as 'taller' or 'shorter' to compare heights

Counting to 10 objects

Using measuring tapes

Rock pools

In this activity, children use small plastic containers to make their own individual rock pools. They arrange rocks (small stones and pebbles), sea creatures and seaweed cut out from dressmaking net and pieces of green or brown plastic bags. When they have counted the number of pots of water and measured the water into their pool, together discuss where they have placed everything in their rock pool, using positional language. Children then measure the width and depth of their pools, recording the results.

You need

- Shallow plastic containers for each child
- Small stones and pebbles
- Plastic sea creatures
- Dressmaking net
- Small pieces of green or brown plastic bags
- A jug of water and yogurt pots for measuring water
- Rulers and measuring tapes

Things to ask

How many pots of water do you think you need to put in your rock pool?

Where do you want the water to come up to in your pool?

What did you decide to put under the rock?

Look, listen, note

Which children can

- decide how many pots of water it will take to fill their rock pool?
- talk about where they placed different objects?
- discuss the depth of water in their pool?

Challenge

Children cooperate with others to make a large rock pool, using a builder's tray.

Children make a list of equipment used in making a large rock pool.

Words to use

how many?, one, two, three ... ten, full, empty, enough, too much, total, altogether, next to, under, on top of, in front of, beside

Maths learning

Shape and space, measures

Using the vocabulary of capacity

Using positional words

Justifying decisions

Fishing

Fill a paddling pool with water and float some small plastic balls in two colours in the pool. Provide fishing nets for the children to try and scoop out the balls. Encourage them to count each scoop of balls separately and decide how many of each colour they caught, and how many altogether. Children could record their fishing totals on a flip chart. For safety reasons, you need to supervise this activity.

Things to ask

I wonder how many balls you will fish out?

How did you decide which colour ball you had the most of?

How many balls did you fish altogether?

Look, listen, note

Which children can

- make a realistic estimate of how many balls they will catch?
- find their total number of balls fished?
- explain a strategy for deciding which colour ball they have the most?

Challenge

Children use three different-coloured balls in the pool.

Children write numbers to 5 on lots of different-coloured balls and fish a set of numbers from 1 to 5 from the pool.

Words to use

one, two, three ... ten, count, most, more, less, fewer, altogether, total

Maths learning

Calculating

Using the language of addition and subtraction

Finding the total number of balls by counting

Comparing two groups of objects

Market traders

Children always role-play their real-life experiences, what they know and where they have been, and then adapt them to suit the new situation. Children need an amount of time to negotiate roles, select props and act out scenarios. As an adult, you can enrich the role play mathematically by becoming a low-key coplayer, modelling how to use some of the props and making observations such as: "I wonder if there are enough hats for everyone?"

Maths learning chart

Maths content

Activities	Page	Number	Calculating	Shape and space	Measures	Problem solving
Flower-and-plant stall	32	●	●			●
Fruit-and-vegetable stall	33	●			●	●
Baker's stall	34		●			●
Ice-cream stall	35	●	●			●
Café stall	36	●	●			●
Seaside stall	37		●	●		●

Problem solving identified

Activities

Problem solving	Flower-and-plant stall	Fruit-and-vegetable stall	Baker's stall	Ice-cream stall	Café stall	Seaside stall
Solving problems	●	●	●	●	●	●
Representing	●	●	●	●	●	
Decision making		●	●	●	●	
Reasoning				●		●
Communicating	●		●			●

Making the most of your market traders role play

Encourage the group to help collect resources for the market traders role play: trailer, barrow, table; artificial turf; dressing-up clothes; till, real money; wooden play food, real food; baskets, paper bags, crates; plates, cups.

Developing a learning conversation

What do you need to do first?

What do you think people prefer to buy: apples or pears?

Where would you need to go to buy one of those objects?

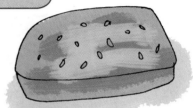

Using ICT to support maths

Card-swiping machine

Calculator

Electronic till

Maths toolkit

Real coins, counters, purse, number line, number fans, interlocking cubes, balance scales, weighing scales

Books to read

The Elephant and the Bad Baby by Elfrida Vipont and Raymond Briggs (Puffin Books)

Benedict Goes to the Beach by Chris Demarest (Picture Ladybird)

Songs to sing

Polly put the kettle on

Five currant buns in the baker's shop

The Queen of Hearts, she made some tarts

Music to listen to

A Tisket, a Tasket by Ella Fitzgerald

Wouldn't it be Lovely by Julie Andrews

Rhapsody in Blue by George Gershwin

Flower-and-plant stall

In this role play, children set up a stall selling flowers and plants. Together, brainstorm about occasions when you buy flowers and discuss the care of flowers and plants. Show children, and encourage them to rehearse how florists wrap a bunch of flowers. Introduce the idea of 'buy one flower, get one free' and demonstrate how to group and count the flowers in twos. You may want to talk about doubling as a strategy for finding out how many flowers customers would get.

You need

- A table for the stall
- Artificial flowers (made or bought) and potted plants (real or artificial)
- Vases
- Price labels
- A cash till and real money
- A receipt pad
- Wrapping paper and ribbon
- Scissors

Things to ask

Can you tell me how much the red flowers cost?

Do you know a way I can work out how many flowers I can buy for 10p?

Will I get change?

Look, listen, note

Which children can

- count out 10 flowers?
- read numerals on price labels?
- count flowers in twos?

Challenge

Introduce additional services such as flower delivery and write a rota for delivery drivers.

Children count how many flowers are growing in the outdoor area and draw a map of their position.

Words to use

count, one, two, three ... ten, how many?, altogether, cost, penny, pence

Maths learning

Number, calculating

Counting objects to 10

Recognising numerals to 9

Counting repeated groups of the same size

Fruit-and-vegetable stall

Children set up a stall selling fruit and vegetables. The vegetables should be real so that children experience the weight, size and texture of different fruit and vegetables. To familiarise children with the produce, instigate a 'stall staff' training day. Demonstrate using scales and balances. Depending on the time of year, introduce and identify, for example, different citrus fruits. Compare the size of a grapefruit with a satsuma and focus on the shape, the weight and the colour.

Things to ask

How many potatoes can I buy for £1?

How much do your oranges weigh?

How large are the cabbages?

Look, listen, note

Which children can

- count out 10 potatoes?
- use weighing apparatus competently?
- talk about vegetables, using weight words such as 'heavy' or 'light'?

Challenge

Children make a chart of everyone's favourite fruit.

Children make vegetable soup for everyone to eat.

Words to use

count, one, two, three ... ten, weight, heavy, heavier, light, lighter, balance, large, larger, small, smaller

Maths learning

Number, measures

Counting objects to 10

Using the language of measurement

Comparing weights

Baker's stall

Children set up a baker's stall that sells rolls and bread. Buy a variety of different shapes and sizes of uncut loaves and paint them with watered-down PVA glue. Make pretend bread rolls from salt dough. Consider the different sizes, shapes and weights of the loaves, agree the price of each loaf and write a label. Suggest the children count the rolls into bags of twos, fours and sixes. Talk about how much each bag would cost and write a price list on the wipe board. Support the children in deciding what they would do if, for example, a customer wanted 8 rolls or 5 rolls. For health-and-safety reasons, discuss with the children the importance of not eating the pretend or painted bread.

You need

- A table for the stall
- An assortment of real loaves painted with watered-down PVA glue
- 20 bread rolls made from salt dough
- Price labels
- Paper bags
- A wipe board and pen
- A cash till and till roll to write receipts
- Real money
- Aprons and hats

Things to ask

Is it possible to buy 6 rolls in two bags?

Can you tell how much those two loaves are altogether?

If I buy three bags with two rolls in each, will that be enough for 6 people?

Look, listen, note

Which children can

- find the sum of two numbers?
- count repeated groups of the same size?
- use different strategies to work out a calculation?

Challenge

Children change the number of rolls in each bag.

Children add 1p to the price of bread and cakes.

Words to use

count, how many?, how much?, total, altogether, one more, one fewer, one, two, three … ten

Maths learning

Calculating

Using the vocabulary involved in adding and subtracting

Beginning to relate addition to combining two groups of objects

Selecting two groups of objects to make a given total

Ice-cream stall

Children set up and operate an ice-cream stall. To resource the stall, children glue together cotton-wool balls and paper cones to make ice-cream cornets that have a mixture of one, two and three scoops (cotton balls) of ice cream. Demonstrate how to construct a cone from a circle by cutting from the edge to the centre. Make ice lollies with wooden sticks and cardboard cut-outs and use small, empty water bottles and drink cartons. Talk to the children about how to price the ice-cream cornets according to how many scoops of ice cream there are.

You need

- A table for the stall
- Coloured cotton-wool balls (ice cream) and brown paper circles (cones)
- Glue and sticking tape
- Lolly sticks and coloured card
- Empty water bottles and drink cartons
- A cash till and real pennies

Things to ask

What do you think the difference between the cost of one-scoop and two-scoop ice-cream cones should be?

I wonder how you work out the cost of two lollies?

About how many drinks have you sold today?

Look, listen, note

Which children can

- explain how they worked out the cost of two items?
- talk about adding and taking away, using pennies?
- make sensible estimates?

Challenge

Children make an ice-cream calculator strip that shows the cost of one cone, two cones, three cones, and so on.

Children double the price of ice lollies.

Words to use

number, count, amount, price, total, altogether, money, penny, pence, add, take away, difference, more, less

Maths learning

Number, calculating

Saying and using number names

Using the vocabulary involved in adding and subtracting

Estimating and using own methods to work through a problem

Café stall

Children set up a food stall with a few tables and chairs next to it. Encourage the children to gather together toy food or use pretend items such as sandwiches and baguettes, sausages, chips, beans, burgers either as a takeaway or to eat 'in the café'. Discuss writing a price list on the wipe board and demonstrate using the calculator and issuing receipts.

You need

- A table for the stall, plus a few additional tables and chairs
- Toy or pretend food
- Open/closed signs
- A wipe board and pen
- Menus and a price list
- A cash till and real money
- A calculator
- A receipt pad
- Aprons and hats

Things to ask

How much does a sandwich and a drink cost?

Can you share that number of biscuits onto two plates?

Is there anything I can buy for 10p?

Look, listen, note

Which children can

- count out an amount of food from a larger group?
- share food equally onto two plates?
- find totals and say how much items cost altogether?

Challenge

Children add more items and their cost to the menu.

Children reduce the prices of food sold as takeaway food.

Words to use

how many?, cost, price, money, pennies, total, double, half, share

Maths learning

Number, calculating

Counting to 10 everyday objects

Sharing objects into equal groups

Using the language of calculation

Seaside stall

Children collect items and make things to put together a stall selling things to use at the beach. Put up a large parasol above the stall. Talk to the children about sorting the shells and selling them in bags of five. Talk about whether the bags should contain shells all the same size or a mixture of sizes and what price the shells should sell for. Rehearse counting in fives. Price other items on the stall and show two clock faces with the opening and closing time of the stall.

Things to ask

How many shells are you putting in the bags?

Can you think of a quicker way to count the shells?

Can you explain why you have grouped those shells together?

Look, listen, note

Which children can

- count the shells into equal groups?
- explain how they know there is the same number of shells in each bag?
- discuss how they have sorted the shells?

Challenge

Children bag up and price beach pebbles.

Children make some beach windmills to sell.

Maths games zone

Participating in games can make maths meaningful for children, so setting up maths games or sporting games outdoors is a good way for children to learn maths in an action-packed way. It gives children an opportunity to jump along number tracks, roll large dice and calculate scores. Playing games also means children are not only practising physical skills such as throwing, hopping and skipping but also talking a lot of maths.

Maths learning chart

Maths content

Activities	Page	Number	Calculating	Shape and space	Measures	Problem solving
Sock it!	40	●				●
Torchlight	41	●				●
Toy track	42	●	●			●
Number crash	43	●	●			●
Shape skip	44			●		●
Moving gloop	45	●			●	●

Problem solving identified

Activities

Problem solving	Sock it!	Torchlight	Toy track	Number crash	Shape skip	Moving gloop
Solving problems				●		●
Representing			●			●
Decision making	●	●	●	●	●	
Reasoning		●		●	●	●
Communicating	●	●	●	●	●	●

Making the most of your maths games zone

Resourcing the maths games zone

Encourage the group to help collect resources for the games zone: large dice, wooden spinners; large number cards; playground chalk; number tracks; skittles, hoops.

Developing a learning conversation

Can you tell me about the game you were playing?

What were the fewest jumps you did in one go?

Can you think of another way to play the game?

Using ICT to support maths

Stopwatch to time how long it takes to play a game

Calculator programmed to act as random dice

Programmable toy to mark out a route

Maths toolkit

Sand timers, measuring tapes, dice, number cards, score boards, number tracks, interlocking cubes, wipe board and pen, easel and board

Books to read

Goal! by Colin McNaughton (Picture Lions)

Hit the Ball, Duck by Jez Alborough (HarperCollins)

The Secret Path by Nick Butterworth (Picture Lions)

Songs to sing

Here we go round the mulberry bush

Two little dicky birds

In and out the dusky bluebells

Music to listen to

Maple Leaf Rag by Scott Joplin

Three Lions by Lightning Seeds

100 Metres by Vangelis from the film *Chariots of Fire*

Sock it!

In this game, children aim to throw rolled-up socks into buckets. Young children's throwing skills are just developing, and they delight in aiming rolled-up socks which are small enough to fit into their hands and which do little harm if they are off target. Children take it in turns to throw five sock balls towards buckets laid on their sides and then count how many are in each bucket.

You need

- Five sock balls made from rolled-up socks
- Three different-coloured buckets laid on their side

Things to ask

Can you explain how to play the game?

How can we find out how many sock balls are in the orange bucket?

I wonder which colour bucket has the most sock balls?

Look, listen, note

Which children can

- count the number of sock balls in each bucket?
- explain how to play the game?
- say which colour bucket contained the most sock balls?

Challenge

Children record the number of sock balls in each bucket on a chart.

Children number the buckets and pick up a number card for each ball in that bucket.

Words to use

zero, one, two ... five, how many?, count, more, most, fewer

Maths learning

Number

Using some number names

Counting reliably to 5 objects

Using language to compare quantities

Torchlight

This game is best if it is played outside on a dull or overcast day or played in a shaded part of the outdoor area. Hang number labels at child height on a fence with as much space between each label as possible and chalk a large circle on the ground a short distance away. Children stand in the circle. One child shines the torchlight onto to one of the numbers, and the rest of the group shouts out the number. Everybody then moves in different ways such as giant strides, hopping, marching or running towards the numeral. They touch the numeral and go back to the circle. Then it is another child's turn to shine the torch.

You need

- 1–10 large number labels
- Playground chalk
- A torch

Things to ask

How did you know it was a 6 that was lit by the torch?

What number is between 5 and 7?

Can you describe where 4 is positioned on the number line?

Look, listen, note

Which children can

- use number language in talk?
- recognise numerals 1 to 10?
- describe a number's position in relation to other numbers?

Challenge

All the children in the group have a torch and shine it on the number that is called.

Extend the number line to 20.

Words to use

numeral, number, one, two, three … ten, next, to, between, before, after

Maths learning

Number

Saying and using number names

Recognising numerals to 10

Identifying the position of a number on a line

Toy track

During this game, children collect pennies by rolling a 1–6 dice and buying soft toys sitting on a number track. Ask the children to put a price label from 1p to 10p on all the toys and to put the labelled toys in the right place on the track: for example, a 1p toy goes on 1, a 5p toy goes on 5, and so on. Put the box of pennies by the track. Children take it in turns to roll the dice and say the number. They take that many pennies from the box and put them in their dish. When they have collected enough pennies, they buy a toy and pay the right amount of pennies into the box. Keep playing until everyone has bought a toy or play longer until the children have bought all the toys.

You need

- A large chalked 1–10 number track
- 10 soft toys
- 10 sticky notes with 1p to 10p written on
- A box of pennies
- A spotty 1–6 dice
- A small penny-collecting dish for each child

Things to ask

How many pennies have you collected?

How many have you rolled on the dice?

How do you know how much a toy costs?

Look, listen, note

Which children can

- recognise dot patterns on the dice?
- count the pennies to find the total?
- use language such as 'more' and 'not enough' during talk?

Challenge

Ask the children to write the price labels.

Include 2p coins with the pennies.

Words to use

one, two, three … ten, how many?, collect, cost

Maths learning

Number, calculating

Counting reliably to 10 everyday objects

Using language to compare amounts

Finding the total number of pennies

Number crash

Children play this game in pairs across a grid. The aim is to get all three cones from one side of the grid to the other before your partner does. You need a large, chalked, horizontal 8 by 3 grid made up of squares. Write 'Start' and 'Finish' on either side of the grid. Children start on opposite sides of the grid and put their cones on the 'Start'/'Finish' space, one cone next to each row. They play with a dice each and take it in turns to roll their dice and move a cone that many spaces along a row. If two cones stop on the same square, there is a number crash. Both players then roll their dice, and the one who rolls the highest number 'wins' the number crash and can stay on the square; the other player's cone goes back to the start. The first player to get all their cones safely to the end of the row onto the 'Finish' space is the winner.

You need

- Playground chalk
- Six PE cones or skittles in two different colours (three of each)
- Two large dotty dice

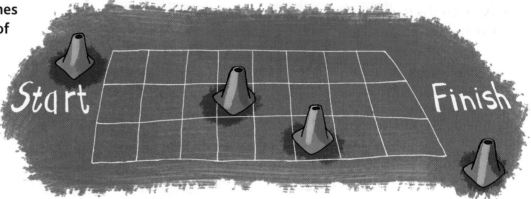

Things to ask

How many spaces along the grid are you going to move?

Can you explain how you knew your dice number was more than your partner's?

If you both roll the same number, have you decided what to do?

Look, listen, note

Which children can

- count along the grid correctly?
- compare two dice numbers and say which is 'more' or 'less'?
- invent a rule for what to do when both players roll the same number in a number crash?

Challenge

Children split the number rolled on their dice between two of their cones.

Children play the game with six cones each and a bigger grid.

Words to use

count, dice, one, two, three ... six, match, how many?, the same, different, more, less, one more, one less

Maths learning

Number, calculating

Recognising dice number patterns

Counting along a grid

Using language such as 'more' or 'less' to compare two numbers

Shape skip

Children play in pairs, one child carrying the shape bag and the other hopping along the pathway. Lay the carpet tiles to make a pathway, Tape one of the shapes onto each tile and arrange the tiles on the pathway in a repeating pattern such as circle, square, triangle, hexagon, circle, square ... To play, the child carrying the bag of shapes takes out a shape and names it; the child on the pathway hops along the tiles until they come to that shape. The child with the bag puts that shape back in the bag and chooses another one. When they have reached the end of the path, they swap roles and hop back the way they came.

Things to ask

How did you decide it was a triangle?

Can you say something about the shape you have picked from the bag?

I wonder what shape you are going to jump to?

Look, listen, note

Which children can

- use the language of shape in talk?
- identify a shape by name?
- explain how they know it is a triangle?

Challenge

Children use a shape dice instead of a shape bag.

Draw 3D shapes on the carpet tiles.

Words to use

shape, circle, square, hexagon, triangle

Maths learning

Shape and space

Using the language of shape

Identifying similarities and differences in shapes

Selecting a particular named shape

Moving gloop

Children play this game in pairs or small teams. Each team has to transfer the 'gloop' in their bowl to an empty bowl a short distance away, using small pots. Each time, they fill up a clean, small pot to the top and then tip it into the empty bowl. Encourage the children to leave the used pot by the empty bowl: that way, they will be able to measure by counting how much 'gloop' they transferred from one bowl to another in a particular time. Using a one-minute sand timer, this game can either be played as three teams racing each other or as pairs seeing how much 'gloop' they can transfer in one minute.

You need

- Three bowls of 'gloop' made from cornflour, food colouring and water in different colours
- Three empty bowls
- Lots of small plastic pots such as yogurt pots or drinking cups
- A sand timer or oven timer

Things to ask

How will you know when your yogurt pot is full?

About how many full yogurt pots of 'gloop' do you think you will be able to move?

Is there more 'gloop' in the first bowl or the second bowl?

Look, listen, note

Which children can

- fill a small pot to the top?
- count how many small pots were filled?
- understand to stop filling when the sand timer runs out?

Challenge

Children fill in a chart to record the amount of 'gloop' they moved.

Children choose another material such as damp sand to move.

Words to use

count, one, two, three … ten, full, empty, how many?, more, fewer

Maths learning

Number, measures

Counting objects to 10

Estimating and comparing quantities

Measuring time using non-standard units

Workbench

Children can use a workbench as an area to make 3D models from technology resources, using the outdoor environment as a stimulus. Provide a variety of tools, materials and equipment for children to experiment with and discuss on a regular basis how to use the different tools. You could encourage the children to turn part of the workbench into a fix-it workshop where they could repair broken models, toys or equipment. It is always useful to locate noisy activities such as hammering outside, but from a safety view, the workbench will need a supporting adult at times.

Maths learning chart

Maths content

Activities	Page	Number	Calculating	Shape and space	Measures	Problem solving
Flying plates	48				★	★
Bunting	49	★		★		★
Nail number line	50	★	★			★
Robot builder	51			★	★	★
Bubbles	52			★	★	★
Picture frames	53			★	★	★

Problem solving identified

Activities

Problem solving	Flying plates	Bunting	Nail number line	Robot builder	Bubbles	Picture frames
Solving problems	★	★	★	★	★	★
Representing			★	★		
Decision making	★	★	★	★	★	★
Reasoning		★	★	★		★
Communicating	★			★		★

Making the most of your workbench

Resourcing the workbench

Encourage the group to help collect resources for the workbench station: construction kits; geoboards and elastic bands; sorting trays; nails, screws, hammers, saws; assortment of woods.

Developing a learning conversation

Can you describe what you are making?

How do you think we could repair this?

I wonder what this tool is used for?

Using ICT to support maths

Light box to illuminate small objects

Glue gun

Digital measure

Maths toolkit

Balance scales, pattern blocks, assorted 2D shapes, plastic mirrors, measuring tapes

Books to read

Fix-It Duck by Jez Alborough (HarperCollins)

The Very Busy Day by Diana Hendry and Jane Chapman (Little Tiger Press)

Harry and the Robots by Ian Whybrow and Adrian Reynolds (Puffin)

What Friends Do Best by Jonathan Emmett and Nathan Reed (HarperCollins)

Songs to sing

Peter hammers with one hammer

London Bridge is falling down

Humpty Dumpty sat on a wall

Music to listen to

Anvil Chorus by Verdi

Symphony Number 5 by Ludwig van Beethoven

Flying plates

Children use the workbench to make kites, using paper plates. Provide each child with a plain paper plate and crayons to draw a pattern on both sides of the plate. Children make tail streamers from thin stripes of crêpe paper of different lengths which they staple to the edge of the plate. Demonstrate how to use the hole punch to make a pair of holes on the opposite edge of the plate for the tail. Children measure and cut 30 centimetres of thin string to thread through the holes. They make the plate fly by running up and down, holding the string and plate high above their heads, and then attaching them by their string to a tree, to watch the tails move in the wind.

You need

- Plain paper plates
- Crayons
- Crêpe paper strips
- A stapler and hole punch
- Thin string
- A few 30 cm rulers
- Scissors

Things to ask

Which of your streamers do you think is the longest?

How did you measure your string?

What did you draw on the reverse side of your plate?

Look, listen, note

Which children can

- use words that refer to length in talk?
- identify the longest streamer?
- discuss how to make a length of string?

Challenge

Children design a different-shaped kite.

Children organise a kite-flying day.

Words to use

long, longer than, short, shorter than, narrow, wide, side, reverse, edge, face, rim

Maths learning

Measures

Using the language of length

Ordering two or three items by length

Describing solutions to practical problems

Robot builder

Children design and make a robot or a new machine. Provide small containers so that the children can sort the nuts, bolts, washers and pieces of wire and other recycled materials such as silver foil and plastic spools before they start building. Introduce a design sheet so that children can draw what they are going to make or have made. Discuss the materials the children are using and their size and shape. Model measuring with rulers and tapes.

Things to ask

What did you decide is the same about the washers?

How tall will your robot be?

Can you explain how you made the legs on your robot the same length?

Look, listen, note

Which children can

- explain the sameness of two objects?
- describe the robot using the language of measures?
- discuss how they made the robot?

Challenge

Attach a robot to another similar programmable toy. Children use it to move the robot round the outside area.

Children write a list of the materials they used to make a robot.

Words to use

how many?, shape, size, measure, tall, taller, short, shorter, wider, wider, light, lighter, heavy, heavier, straight, curved

Maths learning

Shape and space, measures

Sorting objects and identifying similarities and differences

Using language to compare quantities

Talking about methods and choices

Bubbles

Children use mechanical and hand whisks to create bubbles and fill different-sized containers with their own bubbles. Show children and let them handle a range of balloon whisks, including a mechanical one. Examine them carefully and talk about the shape of the whisks and how many strands form the shape. Demonstrate the mechanical whisk, slowly rotating the handle and drawing children's attention to the shape the blades make as they move. Children then choose a whisk to whisk together liquid soap and water to make bubbles. Using spoons to fill containers, the children decide which one holds the most bubbles and which container holds the least.

You need

- Balloon whisks and hand whisk (not electric)
- A range of different-sized containers
- Liquid soap, water
- Spoons

Things to ask

How many spoonfuls of bubbles do you think you could put in this cup?

Why do you think that bowl holds the most bubbles?

Can you describe the way the whisk moves?

Look, listen, note

Which children can

- make observations on the movement of the whisk?
- count the spoonfuls of bubbles into a cup?
- give reasons for their choice of which container holds the most?

Challenge

Children record the results of their findings.

Children make their own bubble frames to blow bubbles through.

Words to use

circle, round, how many?, curve, spoonful, full, empty, handful, holds most, holds least

Maths learning

Shape and space, measures

Using the language of shape and movement

Ordering items by capacity

Making choices and justifying decisions

Picture frames

Children use balsa wood and a glue gun to make a picture frame for a piece of art work they have created. Show the children a variety of different-sized square empty picture frames. Discuss how many sides the frames have and talk about their length. Make sure the children understand that the sides are the same length. Support children as they measure the lengths they need by direct comparison with their pictures and by marking the wood at the saw point. Children put their wood in a vice before sawing the length they need. Demonstrate how to compare the four pieces of sawn wood, making sure they are all the same length. Children glue the four pieces together, using a glue gun. For safety reasons, the children will need to be supervised during this activity. At the end, they use sandpaper to smooth down their frames.

You need

- Narrow balsa wood
- Square empty picture frames
- Measuring tapes
- A vice
- Child saws
- A glue gun
- Sandpaper

Things to ask

How do you know your frame will fit your picture?

Can you explain how you cut the sides the same length?

What shape is your picture frame?

Look, listen, note

Which children can

- say why they know the sides of their frame are the same length?
- discuss how to measure a picture?
- suggest ways to assemble the frame?

Challenge

Children decorate their frame, using a repeating pattern.

Children make a rectangular frame.

Words to use

square, shape, corner, sides, same, different, measure, length, shorter, longer

Maths learning

Shape and space, measures

Using language to describe shape and size of flat shapes and solids

Showing awareness of symmetry

Talking about own ideas, methods and choices

Cooking

Cooking is often one of children's favourite experiences, and there is a wealth of maths learning opportunities to explore, such as weighing ingredients and the changing shape and size of dough as it is kneaded and rolled out. You can make many recipes around a table without the need for an oven, and children will still be able to combine ingredients and use the tools and skills needed for cooking. Cooking also offers a chance to discuss issues concerned with healthy eating.

Maths learning chart

Maths content

Activities	Page	Number	Calculating	Shape and space	Measures	Problem solving
Cracker faces	56	☀		☀		☀
Cookshop	57			☀		☀
Juicing	58		☀		☀	☀
Dough play	59			☀	☀	☀
Choices	60	☀	☀			☀
Gingerbread men	61		☀			☀

Problem solving identified

Activities

Problem solving	Cracker faces	Cookshop	Juicing	Dough play	Choices	Gingerbread men
Solving problems	☀		☀	☀	☀	☀
Representing					☀	
Decision making	☀	☀	☀	☀	☀	☀
Reasoning		☀			☀	☀
Communicating		☀			☀	

Making the most of your cooking area

Resourcing the cooking area

Encourage the group to help collect resources for the cooking area: a range of baking pans and cake tins in different shapes and sizes; patty and tart tins with different numbers of tarts; a range of spoons and stirrers; a selection of pastry cutters; cooking utensils from different cultures.

Developing a learning conversation

I wonder how many pieces of bread you need to make four sandwiches?

How can you make a samosa?

Can you tell us how to cut out that shape?

Using ICT to support maths

Oven timers

Microwave cooker

Digital clock

Maths toolkit

Balance scales, graduated containers, sand timers, number line, measuring tapes

Books to read

I Will Never Not Ever Eat a Tomato by Lauren Child (Orchard Books)

The Tiger Who Came to Tea by Judith Kerr (HarperCollins)

Chocolate Mousse for Greedy Goose by Julia Donaldson and Nick Sharratt (Macmillan Children's Books)

Songs to sing

One potato, two potato

Ten fat sausages

I'm a little teapot

Ten fat peas

Music to listen to

Everybody Eats When They Come to My House by Cab Calloway

The Muffin Man by Ella Fitzgerald

Four Seasons 'Summer' by Vivaldi

Cracker faces

To make cracker faces, children choose a cracker shape, decide whether they want their cracker face to be white, green, pink or brown and spread on the relevant coloured cream cheese. They decorate the face as they wish, choosing straight or curly hair, what to choose as eyes, mouth, and so on. While they are constructing their faces, talk with the children about their choices, the shapes of the items they are using, and how many of each thing they need. Draw children's attention to which of the vegetables have been halved or quartered.

Things to ask

Why did you choose that shape biscuit?

How many potato sticks will you need for the hair?

Why did you decide to use celery for the mouth?

Look, listen, note

Which children can

- count out the various ingredients they need?
- identify by name the shape biscuit they need?
- talk about own choices?

Challenge

Children choose different shapes and make another face, using other ingredients.

Children record the face they made by drawing.

Words to use

shape, square, circle, semicircle, half, quarter, count, one, two, three … six, how many?

Maths learning

Number, shape and space

Saying and using number names

Selecting particular named shapes

Solving practical problems in selecting the appropriate number and size of shapes

Cookshop

Ask the children to help set up a shop selling cooking equipment next to the home corner. Discuss the size and shape of different cooking tools. Talk about why you would need to have different-sized saucepans and bowls. Look at tools for measuring liquids, such as jugs, spoons and cups, as well as weighing scales and balances. Stock the shop with cake tins, baking trays and other items. Together, price everything and set up a till with money.

Things to ask

Can I buy the largest saucepan in the shop?

What do I need to measure milk?

Is there a round cake tin for sale in the shop?

Look, listen, note

Which children can

- organise equipment according to size?
- talk about the difference between particular spoons or such like?
- discuss what items are for sale and how much they cost?

Challenge

Photocopy equipment so that the outline shapes can show where on the shelf to return equipment to.

Children write a price list to display in the shop.

Words to use

small, smaller, smallest, large, larger, largest, circle, curved, round, square

Maths learning

Shape and space

Using language such as 'circle' or 'bigger' to describe the shape and size of objects

Sorting familiar objects to identify their similarities and differences

Ordering items by weight or capacity

Juicing

Take the children on an outing to the local shops or market and buy ingredients for making fruit juice. They use a variety of different-shaped, fruit-squeezing tools to extract the juice. While they are squeezing the fruit, suggest they also focus on comparing how many pips were in each fruit as well as measuring the juice. When they have squeezed all the fruit, children dilute the juice with water and drink it.

You need

- Oranges, grapefruit, satsumas, lemons
- A selection of different types of squeezers for extracting juice by hand
- Drinking water and jugs
- Measuring spoons

Things to ask

How many spoonfuls of juice did you extract from your orange?

Which satsuma had the most pips?

How many pips did you have altogether?

Look, listen, note

Which children can

- discuss the quantity of juice they extracted?
- compare the number of pips collected from different oranges?
- talk about how to find the total number of pips?

Challenge

Children create a block graph by gluing the pips onto squared paper.

Children set up a tasting juice bar and collect data about children's favourite juice drinks.

Words to use

more, less fewer, count, altogether, total, how many?, how much?, full, half full, most, spoonfuls

Maths learning

Calculating, measures

Using language such as 'more' or 'less' to compare two numbers

Using language such as 'greater', 'smaller', 'heavier', 'lighter' to compare quantities

Using the vocabulary involved in adding

Dough play

Children make their own play dough. Give out individual bowls and demonstrate how to measure out a level cup of flour by filling it to the top and smoothing over the top. They then mix together 2 cups of flour and 1 cup of salt in their bowls and stir in some water to make a dough. If a child's dough becomes too sticky, add more flour; if it is too dry, add more water. Children tip their dough onto pastry boards, roll it out and use the cutters to cut out shapes.

Things to ask

How much water did you decide you needed?

How big do you think the dough will be when you roll it out?

I wonder what cutter Jonah used to make that shape?

Look, listen, note

Which children can

- measure the flour successfully?
- describe the size of the dough?
- talk about the shapes that they cut out of the dough?

Challenge

Children make real dough and cut out and bake jam tarts.

Children write a recipe for making dough, detailing how much of each ingredient they need.

Choices

In this activity, children decide whether they prefer apples or satsumas to eat. When they have tasted both fruit, they draw a picture of their preferred fruit on a sticky note. Talk with the children about the two columns of the block graph: one column for those who prefer apples, the other for those who like satsumas. Support children's choices as they stick their label on the correct column of the graph. Together, count and decide the results of the tasting.

You need

• Slices of apple, segments of satsuma
• Sticky notes
• Two-column block graph drawn on a large paper and labelled 'Favourite fruit'

Things to ask

Do you know a way we can find out how many children preferred apples?

How do you know that more children preferred satsumas?

How many children altogether tasted the fruit?

Look, listen, note

Which children can

• count the number of sticky notes in one column accurately?
• make suggestions for how to find the total number of fruit tasters?
• count and compare both columns of the graph to find which has the most?

Challenge

Children display the results of the tasting and write a report for the notice board.

Children choose another two fruits and set up a tasting.

Words to use

count, one, two, three ... ten, more than, less than, total, count, altogether.

Maths learning

Number, calculating

Counting reliably to 10 everyday objects

Using language such as 'more' or 'less' to compare two numbers

Relating addition to combining two groups of objects

Gingerbread men

Encourage the children to do most of the preparation, including weighing all the ingredients. Read the recipe together. Mixing flour and butter, show the children how to rub the butter into the flour and talk about the breadcrumb texture. Weigh the rest of the ingredients and stir into the mixture. Children roll out their own piece of dough on a floured pastry board and cut out different-sized gingerbread men. Before baking, discuss how many gingerbread men the children have made altogether. The mixture makes about 30 gingerbread men. Bake at gas mark 4 for 15 min.

You need

- 350 g plain flour
- 100 g butter
- 175 g soft brown sugar
- 1 egg
- 4 tablespoons golden syrup
- 1 teaspoon bicarbonate of soda
- Half a teaspoon of ginger
- Pastry boards and extra flour for dusting
- Rolling pins
- Gingerbread men cutters in two different sizes
- Baking tray

Things to ask

How many small gingerbread men did you cut out?

How can we find out how many gingerbread men there are altogether?

Did you cut out more large or small gingerbread men?

Look, listen, note

Which children can

- count how many gingerbread men they cut out?
- talk about knowing a way to find the total?
- discuss the difference between the number of small and large gingerbread men?

Challenge

Together, read *The Gingerbread Man* and then share out the baked gingerbread men.

Children zigzag-fold a piece of paper and draw round a gingerbread man cutter. They cut out their drawing to make a line of gingerbread men.

Words to use

count, one, two, three ... ten, how many?, total, altogether, more, less, compare, same as, small, large

Maths learning

Calculating

Using the vocabulary involved in adding

Relating addition to combining two groups of objects

Finding the total number of items in two groups by counting

Dance studio

Assigning an area of your setting as a dance studio is a great way of enabling children to try out movement in a secure environment. Add different resources such as mirrors, scarves and bells to extend the dance. Include music that children and their community are likely to know as well as music with energetic rhythms and quieter, reflective music. Although the area may be small, make sure that there is enough space for children to observe the dancing as some will want to watch before joining in.

Maths learning chart

Maths content

Activities	Page	Number	Calculating	Shape and space	Measures	Problem solving
Follow my leader	64	✦		✦		
Disco dancing	65	✦			✦	
Dancing shoes	66		✦		✦	
Rain dance	67			✦		
Mirror dancing	68			✦		
Dance mats	69			✦	✦	

Problem solving identified

Problem solving	Follow my leader	Disco dancing	Dancing shoes	Rain dance	Mirror dancing	Dance mats
Solving problems		✦	✦		✦	✦
Representing			✦	✦		
Decision making	✦	✦	✦	✦	✦	
Reasoning	✦		✦			
Communicating		✦		✦	✦	✦

Resourcing the dance studio

Encourage the group to help collect resources for the dance studio: a CD player; a selection of different types of dance music; dance mats; dressing-up outfits, scarves, hats; musical instruments; long mirrors.

Developing a learning conversation

Can you tell us about your dance?

How many different steps do you think there are in your dance?

How did you know what direction to dance in?

Using ICT to support maths

CD player

Metronome

Digital camera

Video

Programmable toy

Maths toolkit

Very large 2D shapes, measuring tapes, timers

Books to read

Sometimes I Like to Curl up in a Ball by Vicki Churchill and Charles Fuge (Guillane)

Angelina Ballerina by Helen Craig and Katharine Holdbird (Puffin)

Giraffes Can't Dance by Giles Andrea and Guy Parker Rees (Orchard Books)

Songs to sing

The grand old Duke of York

Dance to your daddy

Music to listen to

Nono Femineh by Ricardo Lemvo and Makina Loca

Invitation to the Dance by Carl Maria von Weber

You Should Be Dancing by The Bee Gees

Follow my leader

Talk to the children about carnival processions and how the procession all follows the same route, one behind the other. Make a route round the dance area by sticking duct tape in a straight line, with some right angles and a square. Walk round the route with the group, pointing out where there are turns in the route and where the square is. Ask the children to dance following a leader along the taped route in time to the music. Encourage them to do the same dance steps as the leader.

You need

- Duct tape
- Music to dance to
- A CD player

Things to ask

Which direction do you need to turn now?

Are there any shapes that you recognise?

Do you need to count any of the steps along the route?

Look, listen, note

Which children can

- suggest ways to dance round the route?
- identify shapes they know?
- count their marching steps accurately?

Challenge

Children use a programmable toy to follow a dance route.

Children draw a route on paper and line up small-world characters along it.

Words to use

number, count, one, two, three ... six, square, triangle, straight, turn, forward, backward, pattern, shape, direction, route

Maths learning

Number, shape and space

Using everyday words to describe position

Using language such as 'square' or 'triangle' to describe shapes

Using number names to talk about dance patterns

Disco dancing

Children work in pairs and put together a sequence of moves to disco music. Together, discuss counting the steps and working together to create a dance routine. Talk about changing direction, dancing low and making different shapes with their bodies. Discuss and rehearse counting in, such as '1, 2, 3, 4', to make sure both dancers start at the same time.

You need

- Disco music
- Disco lights
- A CD player

Things to ask

How many did you count to before you started your dance sequence?

What are the most jumps that you do in your sequence?

Can you explain the pattern of your dance sequence?

Look, listen, note

Which children can

- create a dance sequence of steps and jumps?
- count in the sequence?
- talk about the order in which steps and jumps occur?

Challenge

Children write down their sequence as a number pattern: '3 steps, 1 star jump, 4 moonwalk steps'.

Children teach another pair their dance sequence.

Words to use

one, two, three ... six, turn, direction, repeat, sequence, pattern

Maths learning

Number, measures

Saying and using number names

Counting reliably to 10 everyday objects

Using everyday language related to order and sequence

Dancing shoes

Show children a collection of different types of shoes that are all mixed together. Remove the shoes one at a time and discuss with them the purpose of each shoe, when people would wear them, if they would fit children and their suitability to dance in. Encourage the children to try on the shoes to see if they could use them for dancing. Sort the shoes into two hoops: 'Dancing' and 'Not dancing', according to the children's suggestions. Children pair the shoes in both sets and label the shoes in the 'Dancing' set according to what type of dancing you would use the shoes for.

You need

- A collection of shoes of different types and sizes, including dance shoes
- Two hoops labelled 'Dancing' and 'Not dancing'

Things to ask

Can you guess how many pairs of shoes there are altogether?

What is the same about all the shoes in this hoop?

Are there any shoes smaller than this one?

Look, listen, note

Which children can

- differentiate between the two sets of shoes?
- explain a strategy for finding the total number of pairs of shoes?
- find the shoe lengths by direct comparison?

Challenge

Children draw a recording of their sorting.

Children put together a dance-shoe display, labelling the type of dancing each pair could be used for.

Words to use

counting in twos, two, four, six, eight, ten, how many?, more, less, pair, total, altogether, same different, sort, big, bigger than, small, smaller than

Maths learning

Calculating, measures

Counting repeated groups of the same size

Finding the total number of items in two groups by counting all of them

Sorting familiar objects to identify their similarities and differences

Rain dance

On a rainy day, watch rain falling on different vertical and horizontal surfaces and create a rain scene by using a watering can to water a builder's tray until a puddle forms. Together, brainstorm words about how the rain performs, depending on whether it is falling on a vertical or horizontal surface. Suggest children create rain dances, using rainmaker instruments and wearing cloaks. Talk about twirling, swishing, running and spinning.

Things to ask

Can you describe what happens in your dance?

Did you dance in a straight line or a curved one?

What do you have to do to make the rainmaker work?

Look, listen, note

Which children can

- talk about the dance they created?
- describe the sequence of movements they made?
- explain how to turn the rainmaker?

Challenge

Children make a zigzag book with drawings of their rain-dance sequence.

Children choose a different instrument and create a sunshine dance.

Words to use

turn, spin, circle, horizontal, vertical, roll, run

Maths learning

Shape and space

Talking about and recognising patterns in dance

Using the language of shape and movement

Using everyday words to describe position

Mirror dancing

Set up long mirrors in the dance-studio area or line one of the walls with tin foil so that the children can dance to music and watch their reflection as they practise different steps and arm movements. Next, ask children to dance in pairs, with one child being the dancer and the other the reflection of the dancer. The children then change roles. Together, they discuss the differences in the two dances.

You need

- Mirrors or tin foil
- Music of the children's choice

Things to ask

Which steps did you repeat in your dance?

I wonder if you will raise your arms up high in your dance?

How difficult was it to reflect Sami's dance?

Look, listen, note

Which children can

- create and repeat dance steps to make a pattern?
- discuss the dance routine?
- attempt to reflect another child's action?

Challenge

Children create a pair dance with the same moves.

Film the dances. Children then watch and comment on the movements they made.

Words to use

above, below, high, low, in front of, next to, behind, repeat, same, different, opposite

Maths learning

Shape and space

Using everyday words to describe position

Talking about patterns of dance

Showing awareness of symmetry

Dance mats

Provide children with dance mats on which to perform a dance that lasts for a minute. Talk about using the whole of the mat for their dance. Children listen to fast and slow dance music for a minute each. Use the one-minute sand timer and make sure that the children understand that both pieces of music lasted for the same amount of time. Children each decide whether they want to dance to fast or slow music. They rehearse their dances on the mats, using lots of different steps, turns and jumps, including lying down.

You need

- Rectangular dance mats or yoga mats
- Fast and slow dance music
- A CD player
- A one-minute sand timer

Things to ask

Does your dance cover the whole length of the mat?

Are you dancing to the fast or the slow music?

What does it mean if your dance finishes before the music stops?

Look, listen, note

Which children can

- tell on which part of their mat they perform their dance?
- identify whether their dance is fast or slow?
- explain how the sand timer works?

Challenge

Children create a dance to different music.

Children use different-shaped dance mats such as circles.

Words to use

fast, slow, minute, time, timer, turn, forward, back, sideways, pattern, length, width, edge, centre, end, before, after, too short, too long

Maths learning

Shape and space, measures

Using everyday words to describe position

Talking about and creating dance patterns

Using everyday language related to time

'Hands-on' station

The 'hands-on' station is about exploring materials and learning through practical experience to develop ideas and skills. It provides an opportunity for children to handle different textures, while being involved in messy play at times, and offers various sensory experiences. Children can use maths language and apply maths knowledge such as problem solving and measuring, estimating and sequencing.

Maths learning chart

Maths content

Activities	Page	Number	Calculating	Shape and space	Measures	Problem solving
Compost digging	72		●			●
Exploring tea leaves	73			●		●
A scoop of rice	74	●			●	●
Play-dough snakes	75	●			●	●
Papier-mâché modelling	76			●		●
Sticky stuff	77			●	●	●

Problem solving identified

Activities

Problem solving	Compost digging	Exploring tea leaves	A scoop of rice	Play-dough snakes	Papier-mâché modelling	Sticky stuff
Solving problems	●	●	●		●	●
Representing		●				
Decision making		●		●	●	●
Reasoning	●		●	●		
Communicating			●			●

Making the most of your 'hands-on' station

Resourcing the hands-on' station

Encourage the group to collect equipment for the 'hands-on' station: cutters; bubble mixture; squirters; airtight containers; pastry boards, bowls; jars, labels; bubble wrap; flour, food colouring.

Developing a learning conversation
Can you describe how it felt?
How could you change the shape of your dough?
Can you explain how you measured your bubble?

Using ICT to support maths
Electronic weighing machine
Calculator
Computer-writing programme

Maths toolkit
Rulers, measuring tapes, 2D shapes and 3D solids, numerals, sorting materials, plastic mirrors

Books to read
Jasper's Beanstalk by Nick Butterworth and Mick Inkpen (Hodder and Stoughton)
Kids by John Burningham (Red Fox)

Songs to sing
My hands upon my head I place
Tommy Thumb
Ten little fingers
Jelly on a plate

Music to listen to
Wonderful World by Louis Armstrong
Pastoral Symphony by Ludwig van Beethoven

Compost digging

Children use compost and small gardening tools to fill and empty flowerpots. If you set up the compost in a sand tray and bury plastic minibeasts in it, children can dig for them. When they have dug up some minibeasts, model and discuss with the children scenarios where four minibeasts are hiding in a flowerpot and one escapes. Talk about how many minibeasts might be left in the flowerpot and each time reveal the answer. Encourage children to ask each other questions about the number of minibeasts, including minibeasts joining existing groups in the flowerpots.

You need

- A large bag of compost
- Child-sized gardening tools
- Small flowerpots
- An empty sand tray or other deep container
- Plastic minibeasts

Things to ask

How many minibeasts have you found altogether?

If one minibeast escapes, how many will there be left in the flowerpot?

Supposing another beetle creeps into your flowerpot, how many will be in there then?

Look, listen, note

Which children can

- talk about adding and taking away minibeasts?
- respond to several questions?
- discuss and use minbeasts to support their answers?

Challenge

Children use drawings to record totals for escaping minibeasts.

Children hide minibeasts and then dig them up and record as they do so.

Words to use

add, altogether, total, one more, one less, how many, how many more, take away, subtract

Maths learning

Calculating

In practical activities, use the vocabulary involved in adding and subtracting

Finding 'one more' or 'one less' than a number to 10

Beginning to relate addition to combining two groups of objects and subtraction to 'taking away'

Exploring tea leaves

Children use a builder's tray filled with tea leaves to explore shape patterns. Tea leaves are a good medium to use: apart from the tactile experience of grabbing handfuls of dried leaves and letting them go, the leaves will usually hold a drawn shape until the tray is shaken or raked over. Encourage the children to draw patterns, using a range of different drawing tools.

You need

- A builder's tray
- Loose tea leaves (unused)
- Small rakes
- African combs
- Small twigs and sticks

Things to ask

Can you tell me about your pattern?

How did you make those lines so straight?

Did you create any shapes in your pattern? Which ones?

Look, listen, note

Which children can

- describe the pattern they have created?
- talk about using rakes and combs to draw lines?
- discuss drawing shapes or using space in their pattern?

Challenge

Children use utensils of their choice to draw patterns.

Children use the tea leaves to fill small containers, using teaspoons.

Words to use

pattern, shape, line, corner, straight, curved, spiral, circle, square

Maths learning

Shape and space

Talking about pattern

Using the language of shape and space

Showing awareness of symmetry

A scoop of rice

Children explore ideas about capacity by using the pouring quality of rice. Let children investigate pouring and playing with the rice, then demonstrate how to use a scoop by filling it and levelling the top. Choose a small container such as a cup to count the scoopfuls into and make sure the children understand that the scoop has to be full and then levelled off. Next, choose two containers, one tall and one wide, and discuss with the children which container will hold the most rice. Challenge them to find out which one holds the most.

Things to ask

How will you know when the scoop is full?

Can you explain how you know that jar holds the most?

How many scoopfuls will the box hold?

Look, listen, note

Which children can

- successfully count their scoopfuls into a container?
- explain a strategy for finding out which item holds the most?
- talk about capacity?

Challenge

Children order three items by comparing capacities.

Children record their results by drawing.

Play-dough snakes

Children experiment with salt dough. Demonstrate to the children how to make dough snakes by first rolling a piece of dough into a small ball and then rolling the ball with two hands backward and forward to make a snake. When they have made several snakes, children compare the snakes' lengths and decide which snake is the longest and which the shortest. Suggest to the children to turn the snakes into numerals.

You need

- 3 cups flour, 1 cup salt, 1 cup water, green food colouring
- Rolling pins, pastry boards

Things to ask

Can you make a snake longer than this one?

How can we find out which snake is the shortest?

What number will you turn your snake into?

Look, listen, note

Which children can

- use length words during talk?
- use a strategy to find the longest or shortest snake?
- identify numerals to 9?

Challenge

Children bake the salt-dough numbers in the oven. When the numbers are cool, they paint and varnish them.

Children assemble the snake numerals as a number line.

Words to use

length, long, longer, longest, short, shorter, shortest, the same as, number numeral, one, two, three … nine

Maths learning

Number, measures

Using the language of length

Ordering items by length

Recognising numerals 1 to 9

Papier-mâché modelling

Children create landscape models. They first tear newspapers into strips and put them in a bucket with watered-down PVA glue. They then construct a landscape in twos and threes by arranging small pots and boxes onto a large cardboard base. Show the children how to change the height of their landscape by turning a box on its side or standing one thing on top of another and discuss where things are positioned. When children are satisfied with their arrangement, they cover everything, including the base, with the newspaper strips. Finally, they paint the whole landscape construction with more watered-down glue and leave it to dry.

Things to ask

What shaped boxes are you going to choose for your model?

Are you going to put anything next to that cylinder?

Have you decided whether to make your box taller?

Look, listen, note

Which children can

- identify the shape they are using?
- talk about the position of their their boxes?
- describe what they are constructing?

Challenge

Children paint their model landscapes when they have dried.

Children arrange small-world characters on their landscapes.

Sticky stuff

Individually, children mix together flour, baby oil and food colouring to make a sticky mixture that they can roll into balls. Encourage them to tip a scoop of flour onto a board and drip oil and food colouring onto it. Show how to stir the measured mix until it begins to stick together and form a ball. Children cover their hands in flour and use them to turn the ball into different 3D shapes.

You need

- Flour
- Baby oil
- Food colouring
- Measuring spoons, cups and scoops
- Spoons and stirrers
- A builder's tray or small chopping boards

Things to ask

Do you think the ball you made is larger or smaller than a football?

How did you measure the flour?

Can you explain how you made your ball change into a sausage?

Look, listen, note

Which children can

- talk about measuring the flour and oil?
- identify or name the properties of the shapes they made?
- discuss how they decided what shapes to make?

Challenge

Children take a photo of each of the stages of making sticky stuff.

Children put the photos in order and turn them into a book.

Words to use

measure, full, empty, more than, less than, longer than, shorter than, bigger than, smaller than, shape, cylinder, long, wide

Maths learning

Shape and space, measures

Using language to describe the shape and size of solids

Using the language of capacity

Talking about own ideas, methods and choices

Maths workshop

Using puzzles and games and exciting maths activities give children the opportunity to engage with maths as a creative subject. The maths workshop should be an inviting place for the children to play, where they can select their own maths resources to explore, as well as join in with and adapt planned experiences. Working as a pair or in a small group often means that children can tackle more challenging maths. Use the workshop to show children how to play a board game and then leave it for them to develop and change.

Maths learning chart

Maths content

Activities	Page	Number	Calculating	Shape and space	Measures	Problem solving
Colour move	80	✹				✹
Our calendar	81	✹			✹	✹
More or less	82	✹	✹			✹
I spy numbers	83	✹				✹
Sort it!	84		✹	✹	✹	✹
Marbles	85		✹			✹

Problem solving identified

Activities

Problem solving	Colour move	Our calendar	More or less	I spy numbers	Sort it!	Marbles
Solving problems	✹	✹	✹	✹	✹	✹
Representing		✹				
Decision making		✹		✹	✹	✹
Reasoning	✹		✹	✹		
Communicating			✹			✹

Making the most of your maths workshop

Resourcing the maths workshop

Encourage the group to help collect resources for the maths workshop: peg boards; dice games, card games, board games, dominoes, jigsaw puzzles; sorting materials.

Developing a learning conversation

How do you think the pattern carries on?

Can you tell me how you worked out what to do?

Can you say how you know which ones are missing?

Using ICT to support maths

Calculator

Photocopier to photocopy constructions

Computer-drawing package

Maths toolkit

Dice, spinners, number cards, number lines, number tracks, measuring equipment, cubes, beads, counting cubes

Books to read

One Ted Falls out of Bed by Anna Currey (Macmillan Children's Books)

Contrary Mary by Anita Jeram (Walker Books)

Ten Terrible Dinosaurs by Paul Stickland (Ragged Bears Publishing Ltd)

Songs to sing

There were 10 in the bed

1, 2, buckle my shoe

1, 2, 3, 4, Mary at the cottage door

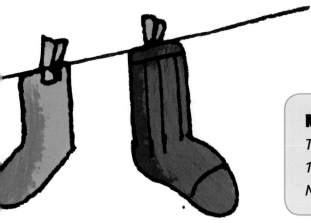

Music to listen to

The Entertainer by Scott Joplin

1-2-3 by Gloria Estefan and the Miami Sound Machine

Moonlight Sonata by Ludwig van Beethoven

Colour move

In this non-competitive activity, children move a dinosaur along a track, and it is the dinosaur that wins or loses, not the child. Children take it in turns to roll a coloured dice and move that colour dinosaur one square along the track towards the dinosaur house. The winner is the first dinosaur to reach the house.

Things to ask

How can we find out how many squares before the blue dinosaur reaches home?

Which colour dinosaur was second to reach home?

Why do you think the red dinosaur will be the first to reach home?

Look, listen, note

Which children can

- count the squares to find how many?
- use ordinal words correctly?
- explain ideas about turn-taking and dinosaur moves?

Challenge

Children use more dinosaurs, number them and use a number dice.

Children roll a colour dice and a dotty dice together. They move that colour dinosaur shown on the colour dice the number of squares shown on the dotty dice.

Words to use

forward, first second, third, last, one, two, three ... ten

Maths learning

Number

Counting objects to 10

Using ordinal number words

Developing mathematical ideas

Our calendar

Children look at a large calendar and write sticky notes to put on the calendar to identify special days, outings, school happenings and visitors who are coming. Together, discuss how the current month of the calendar is organised. Draw children's attention to the days from Monday to Friday. Count how many days to the next birthday, celebration or other occasion. Children look at the weekend days together, say the names of the days and count how many weekends there are in the whole month. They put their own written sticky notes on the calendar day that is important to them and the community.

Things to ask

How many days in a week do you come to school?

How can we find out how many days before the puppet show?

Can you see any numbers on the calendar that you know?

Look, listen, note

Which children can

- talk about the days of the week?
- count the days between two events?
- identify some numerals on the calendar?

Challenge

Children write a weekly diary of events for the notice board.

Children keep a weekly weather chart.

More or less

Children work in pairs to decide who has more or fewer pennies. Each child needs 5 pennies in a purse. They choose to take out as many or as few pennies as they want to. Both children line up their pennies and say how many are in their own line. Flip the 'more/less' 2p coin. If the coin lands on 'more', the child who has lined up more pennies wins a prize. If the coins lands on 'less', the child who has lined up fewer coins wins a prize. Both children put their pennies back in their purses, and each child chooses a different number of pennies to line up. Keep playing until both children have won three prizes.

You need

- 5 pennies in a purse for each child
- A 2p coin labelled 'more' on one side and 'less' on the other
- 10 small-world characters as prizes

Things to ask

Did you take less than 5 pennies out of your purse?

How did you work out who had more pennies?

What can you do now that you both have the same number of pennies in the line?

Look, listen, note

Which children can

- count their line of pennies and say how many?
- say which line of pennies has more or fewer?
- suggest a way of solving the same number of pennies in the line problem?

Challenge

Increase the number of pennies in each purse to 10.

Children use a mixture of 1p and 2p pennies.

Words to use

count, one, two, three ... ten, how many?, total, penny, pence, pennies, more, less, compare, same

Maths learning

Number, calculating

Counting reliably to 10 everyday objects

Using language such as 'more' and 'less' to compare two numbers

Using own methods to work through a problem

I spy numbers

Children take it in turns to feel a wooden numeral in the bag. They name it before removing it and checking. They then take five stickers, look around the room for five examples of the number they took from the bag and put a sticker on each number they find. They describe to the other children where they found their numerals, and in what order they found them.

Things to ask

How did you know it was a 7 in the 'feely' bag?

What other numbers do you think are in the bag?

Can you explain where you spied your first 7?

Look, listen, note

Which children can

- identify a numeral by feel?
- discuss numbers they have seen or know?
- use ordinal language in talk?

Challenge

Children choose another numeral and look for that number.

Children take photos or do rubbings of the found numerals.

Words to use

number, numerals, one, two, three ... ten, first second, last

Maths learning

Number

Recognising numerals 1 to 9

Saying and using number names

Using ordinal numbers

Sort it!

Children sort out and peg socks on a washing line. They take the socks from the washing basket, discuss who might wear particular socks and whether they would be bigger or smaller than themselves. Children then sort the socks, match them into pairs and peg them on the line. When they have pegged up all the socks, children count them in twos and check by counting them again in ones.

Things to ask

How many pairs of socks do you think there are?

Can you explain why you think those two socks are a pair?

Which pair of socks do you think is the biggest?

Look, listen, note

Which children can

- identify two socks that are a pair?
- count pairs of socks in twos?
- discuss the sizes of different socks?

Challenge

Children find the smallest and the largest pair of socks.

Children sort out a collection of gloves.

Words to use

one, two, three ... ten, pair, pattern, size, big, bigger, small, smaller, long, longer, count in twos, 2, 4, 6, 8, 10, add, take away, total

Maths learning

Calculating, shape and space, measures

Matching together similar objects

Counting repeated groups of the same size

Using the language of measurement

Marbles

Children roll marbles around inside plastic dishes and focus on different number combinations. They choose four marbles each, put them in their dish and tip the dish from side to side. In this way, some marbles fall one side of the divider and some the other. When everybody is satisfied with how they have separated their marbles, they share their number combination with the rest of the group. With four marbles there are three possible combinations (4/0, 3/1 and 2/2), although the children may not realise this.

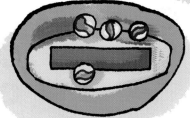

Things to ask

How many marbles have you got altogether?

Does anyone have the same number of marbles on each side?

Who has a different number of marbles on each side?

Look, listen, note

Which children can

- work out what the number combination would be if a marble rolled to the other side of the dish?
- compare the number of marbles either side of the dish?
- say how many marbles there are altogether?

Challenge

Children record all the ways that they can separate four marbles in the dish.

Children use a different number of marbles and find out how many ways they can separate them.

Words to use

one, two, three, four, altogether, total, more than, less than, the same, different, one more than, one less than

Maths learning

Calculating

Knowing that the quantity changes when something is added or taken away

Making comparisons between quantities

Selecting two groups to make a given total of objects

Music studio

The rhythm and repetition in music supports young children's maths learning. A music studio makes a lively addition to any early years setting with many enthusiastic players. It is important for children to take part in the creation and production of music and also to have the opportunity to listen to music. Making music can be noisy, so you might want to organise this in a quiet corner that you can curtain off with a blanket to muffle the sound of the band rehearsal a little!

Maths learning chart

Maths content

Activities	Page	Number	Calculating	Shape and space	Measures	Problem solving
Sliding and shaking	88	★		★		★
Up and down	89	★	★			★
Outlines	90			★	★	★
Musical maths box	91	★				★
Sing a song	92		★			★
Nursery rhymes	93	★	★			★

Problem solving identified

Activities

Problem solving	Sliding and shaking	Up and down	Outlines	Musical maths box	Sing a song	Nursery rhymes
Solving problems	★		★	★	★	
Representing			★	★	★	★
Decision making	★	★		★	★	★
Reasoning			★		★	
Communicating	★	★			★	★

Making the most of your music studio

Resourcing the music studio

Encourage the group to collect resources for the music area: home-made shakers, home-made string instruments, a range of different musical instruments, including those from different cultures; sheet music; a CD player and CDs.

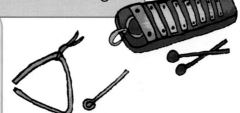

Developing a learning conversation

What would happen if you used a different instrument?

Would it sound different if you played the music slowly?

What patterns did you notice when you were listening?

Using ICT to support maths

CD player

Record player

An electronic instrument

Maths toolkit

Number cards, number lines, 2D shapes, counting cubes

Books to read

So Much by Trish Cook and Helen Oxenbury (Walker Books)

The Very Quiet Cricket by Eric Carle (Penguin Books Ltd)

Songs to sing

When Goldilocks went to the house of the bears

This old man, he played one

Five little ducks went swimming one day

Music to listen to

The Torridor's Song from *Carmen* by Scott Joplin

Tounga by Lightning Seeds

Walkin' Blues by Eric Clapton

The Young Person's Guide to the Orchestra by Benjamin Britten

Sliding and shaking

Some children choose to thread up to 10 curtain rings onto short wooden poles. Other children choose to put 10 cubes into tins with lids. The group then makes sounds by sliding the rings backward and forward on the pole by changing the position of the pole or by shaking or turning the containers in different positions. When the children are confident with this, encourage them to work as an orchestra, using four beats to create a sound pattern: the sliders are using two beats, followed by the shakers shaking tins twice, then the sliders and the shakers again. Experiment with slow and fast sliding and shaking while you count the beat.

You need

- Wooden curtain rings
- A wooden curtain pole cut into 30 cm lengths
- Plastic cubes
- Empty tins with lids

Things to ask

How many rings did you decide to put on your pole?

Can you count the beat for us?

How would you describe the sound pattern?

Look, listen, note

Which children can

- count out a number of rings?
- count aloud, emphasising second beat numbers (1, **2**, 3, **4**)?
- talk about how to make a sound pattern?

Challenge

Children choose a different number of rings.

Introduce a third instrument.

Words to use

count, one, two, three … ten, high, low, fast, slow, pattern, repeat

Maths learning

Number, shape and space

Counting objects to 10

Recreating simple patterns

Using everyday language related to time

Up and down

Children use xylophones and glockenspiels to explore counting forward and backward as they play the instruments' scales up and down. To emphasise counting high and low, they stand the instruments against a wall or hold them vertically while they play them. Children accompany the playing of the full scale with counting from 1 to 10 and back. Encourage them to experiment by starting the count from a number other than 1 and sometimes counting in twos or fives and playing the instruments loud or soft, fast or slow.

You need
- Xylophones
- Glockenspiels
- Beaters

Things to ask

Are you going to choose to count forward or backward?

Who can remember what numbers you say when you count in twos?

What number shall we start the count from now?

Look, listen, note

Which children can

- talk about numbers and their order?
- count to 10 to accompany the music?
- decide whether to count forward or backward?

Challenge

Make a tape recording of the music and the counting.

Children use chime bars instead of glockenspiels.

Words to use

count, number, one, two, three … ten, forward, backward, one more, one less, count in twos, count in fives

Maths learning

Number, calculating

Saying and using number names

Counting forward and backward to 10

Counting in twos and fives to 20

Outlines

Children listen to the sound an instrument makes and identify the instrument from the shape. Arrange four instruments on an overhead projector and put a second set of the same four instruments on a table. Children play some notes on one of the four table instruments, and the rest of the group decides which of the reflected overhead instruments was played. Together, discuss the shape and size of the reflected instruments and strategies for identifying the instrument.

You need

- Two drums
- Two triangles
- Two small xylophones
- Two recorders
- An overhead projector and screen

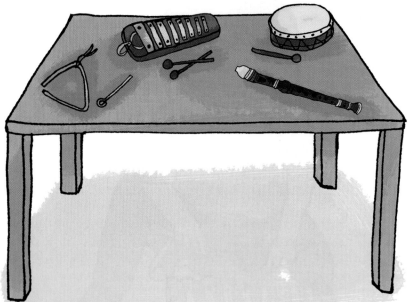

Things to ask

Can you explain why you think that shape is a drum?

What is the narrowest shape you can see?

Can you see a shape that has three sides?

Look, listen, note

Which children can

- identify instruments by their shape?
- use measurement words to describe an instrument?
- talk about why they chose a particular shape?

Challenge

Children choose four other musical instrument shapes to reflect on the overhead projector.

Children make a poster of outlines of musical instruments.

Words to use

circle, triangle, rectangle, side, edge, corner, long, longer, short, shorter, wide, narrow

Maths learning

Shape and space, measures

Matching shapes and objects by recognising similarities and orientation

Using the language of measures

Talking about own ideas and choices

Musical maths box

Children collect together and put in a box some musical instruments, a puppet and other objects such as five plastic frogs, large number cards and anything they could use when they are singing counting rhymes and number songs. They then sing a counting song such as 'Five little monkeys walked along the shore'. They use the instruments in the box and involve the puppet which can make deliberate mistakes for the children to correct. During the song, children holding number cards show them at the relevant point; children holding instruments play them to make the right number of sounds.

You need

- Percussion instruments
- A box
- Objects such as plastic frogs and small-world characters, as part of a counting song
- A puppet
- Large 1–10 number cards

Things to ask

What number do you think comes next?

How many monkeys will be left if one goes for a swim?

Supposing we started with more monkeys, what would we need to do?

Look, listen, note

Which children can

- join in with the number rhyme?
- read the numerals on the cards?
- offer suggestions how to change the numbers in the rhyme?

Challenge

Children act out the number rhyme, using the percussion instruments.

Children choose another number rhyme to dramatise.

Words to use

count, one, two, three ... ten, sequence, counting on, counting back

Maths learning

Number

Saying and using number names in order

Recognising numerals 1 to 9

Using developing mathematical ideas

Sing a song

This traditional song sung to the tune of 'When Johnny comes marching home' is easy for children to sing along to. Children work in pairs and, together, choose 12 dinosaurs which they line up in a single line. They sing the following song:

The animals went in one by one, hurrah, hurrah
The dinosaur eating a currant bun, hurrah, hurrah

The animals went in two by two, hurrah, hurrah
The rhinoceros and the kangaroo, hurrah, hurrah   and so on

As they sing each verse, children regroup their dinosaurs into twos, then threes, fours, and so on. If they cannot make a number such as '5', they either take more dinosaurs or put some back in the box.

Things to ask

How many dinosaurs have you got altogether?

How many groups of three do you think you will make?

Do you need to add or take away any dinosaurs?

Look, listen, note

Which children can

- count a collection of dinosaurs?
- regroup a collection in a particular number?
- work out how many 'more/less' dinosaurs they need to make a particular number?

Challenge

Children make a poster illustrating the song.

Children record themselves singing the song with musical accompaniment.

Words to use

count, one, two, three ... twelve, how many?, total, altogether, more, less, fewer, group

Maths learning

Calculating

Counting repeated groups of the same size

Using language such as 'more' and 'less'

Relating addition to combining groups and subtraction to take away

Nursery rhymes

Everyone in the group sits together and sings a selection of nursery rhymes. At the end of the singing, children suggest which are their favourite nursery rhymes. Put out three hoops each labelled with a nursery rhyme. Children go and stand in the hoop with the nursery rhyme they like best. Together, decide which hoop has the most children standing in it and sing that nursery rhyme again.

Things to ask

How can we find out how many children liked the Humpty Dumpty rhyme?

Does this hoop have more or fewer children than that hoop?

Who can suggest a way of finding out what nursery rhyme most children liked best?

Look, listen, note

Which children can

- count successfully the number of children standing in a hoop?
- describe and compare the number of children standing in two hoops?
- suggest a strategy for finding out the favourite rhyme?

Challenge

Children make a photographic record of children standing in the hoops and write the accompanying labels.

Children ask a larger group their favourite nursery rhyme and compare results.

Words to use

one, two, three ... ten, count, more, most, less, fewer, total, altogether

Maths learning

Number, calculating

Counting to 10 everyday objects

Using 'more' or 'less' to compare two numbers

Using mathematical ideas and methods to solve practical problems

Story tent

Setting up a story tent makes an exciting and inviting way to share stories. With the children's help, you can change the tent by adding different fabrics, colours and resources such as torches, stars or leaves, depending on the stories shared. In the story tent, encourage children to talk about and recall events from the story, using the things that occur in the book as a stepping stone to collecting data on children's likes and dislikes. A story will also often initiate discussion about shape and symmetry and provide a forum for exploring children's ideas about number.

Maths learning chart

Maths content

Activities	Page	Number	Calculating	Shape and space	Measures	Problem solving
Jungle animals	96	●	●			●
Eggs	97				●	●
Rhinoceros	98			●		●
Next thing	99	●				●
What's it like?	100			●		●
Sleeping	101	●				●

Problem solving identified

Activities

Problem solving	Jungle animals	Eggs	Rhinoceros	Next thing	What's it like?	Sleeping
Solving problems	●	●	●	●	●	●
Representing	●		●	●	●	●
Decision making	●	●		●		●
Reasoning		●			●	●
Communicating		●	●		●	

Making the most of your story tent

Resourcing the story tent

Encourage the group to help collect resources for the story tent: cushions; a rug; posters. To make a story tent, you need 25 pieces of 1 cm x 120 cm dowling and gaffer tape. Use 10 pieces of dowling to lay out two pentagons and tape together the five points on each. On the first pentagon, attach two further pieces of dowling to each taped point to make five standing triangle shapes. This forms the lower section of the tent. For the second pentagon, the top of the tent, attach a piece of dowling to each point and attach the other end of those five pieces to the five standing triangles.

Developing a learning conversation

How can we remember what happened?

Have we got enough to make it?

I wonder what this could be a photograph of?

Using ICT to support maths

Tape recorder and headphones

Computer-data package to record books read

Scanner to scan own illustration for the stories

Maths toolkit

Coloured rods, interlocking cubes, number line, number track, measuring tapes, number fans, assorted 2D shapes

Books to read

Beware the Storybook Wolves by Lauren Child (Hodder Children's Books)

Once upon a Time by John Prater (Walker Books)

Each Peach, Pear, Plum by Janet and Allan Ahlberg (Puffin Books)

Songs to sing

The bear went over the mountain

This little piggy went to market

She'll be coming round the mountain when she comes

Music to listen to

Sounds of Silence by Simon and Garfunkel

Peter and the Wolf by Sergei Prokofiev

Piano Concerto No 1 by Franz Liszt

Jungle animals

Read the book aloud in the story tent. The use of repetition makes it an excellent book to use as a starter story for children to continue the story after the book finishes. As you read the story, produce the soft toys that are linked to the story, counting and recounting, using fingers, each time another one is added. When you have finished the story, invite the children to continue the walk through the jungle and count as you get out other soft-toy animals.

You need

- *Walking Through the Jungle* by Julie Lacome (Walker Books)
- Five soft toys or pictures of a snake, a lion, an elephant, a monkey and a crocodile
- Five additional soft toys for children to count in the jungle

Things to ask

How many animals are there in the jungle now?

How many animals will we have if we add 'one more'?

Can you explain what you did to find the total?

Look, listen, note

Which children can

- count the animals accurately?
- explain a strategy for finding the total when one more animal is added?
- talk about adding and taking away animals?

Challenge

Children make a 1–10 number track and put on all the animals that have been counted.

Children draw a jungle picture and outline 10 animals.

Words to use

count, one, two, three ... ten, one more, altogether, total, more than, less than

Maths learning

Number, calculating

Counting reliably to 10 objects

Finding 'one more' or 'one less' than a number from 1 to 10

Beginning to use the vocabulary involved in adding and subtracting

Eggs

The Odd Egg is beautifully illustrated, and with few words and different page sizes, children will soon pick up the emphasis on size. The story is about a group of birds that hatch their eggs and a duck that hatches a crocodile. In the story tent, look at the book with a few children at a time so that they can all see the drawings. Give the children different-sized eggs to handle and discuss. Choose three eggs, talk about them and ask the children to put them in order of size.

You need

- *The Odd Egg* by Emily Gravett (Macmillan Children's Books)
- A collection of different-sized eggs, both real (hard-boiled) and manufactured

Things to ask

How can we find which egg is the largest?

Can you explain why you think that egg is the smallest?

How did you sort your egg collection?

Look, listen, note

Which children can

- make suggestions about the size of the eggs?
- talk about a way of comparing egg size?
- identify a property of their egg sorting?

Challenge

Children cut out different-sized ovoid shapes, decorate them and put them in size order.

Children tie-dye some real eggs by putting elastic bands round the eggs and dipping them in natural food dye.

Words to use

small, smaller, smallest, big, bigger, biggest, large, larger, largest, size, shape, heavier, lighter

Maths learning

Measures

Using language such as 'bigger' to describe objects

Talking about own ideas, methods and choices

Sorting familiar objects to identify similarities and differences

Rhinoceros

Read the storybook, which is full of rhythm, humour and rhyming words, aloud for children to appreciate the effect of the rhythm. It is a story about four friends running away from a rhinoceros, and it uses lots of positional and measurement words such as 'beneath', 'wide' and 'deep'. Ask the children to sit in a circle, and as you read the story, introduce hand movements and gestures to dramatise the positional and measurement words. Encourage the children to join in and contribute their ideas of how they can illustrate some of the words with their hands: for example, pointing behind them or holding their hands far apart to show 'wide'.

You need

- *The Cross-with-us Rhinoceros* by John Bush and Paul Geraghty (Red Fox Picture Books)

Things to ask

How can we show 'deep' and 'wide' with our hands?

Can you tell us what you would do if you saw a rhinoceros following you?

Who can remember what happens when the friends reach the river?

Look, listen, note

Which children can

- suggest ways to show positional words with their hands?
- talk about their ideas for an escaping rhinoceros, such as 'up a tree', 'down a hole', 'run very fast'?
- retell part of the story?

Challenge

Children teach others their hand movements as you read the story.

Children write positional word labels and place them around the room.

Words to use

beneath, wide, deep, high, low, left, right, middle, above, under, behind, in front, first, last

Maths learning

Shape and space

Using everyday words to describe position

Describing solutions to practical problems

Using everyday language related to order and sequence

Next thing

The maths activity based on *Whatever Next!* focuses on using ordinal language early on in the book, where Bear collects items to help him fly to the moon. Read the story in the story tent and reflect with the children on how, where and in what order Bear found what he needed. Show the objects themselves as you discuss them and ask the children to match the ordinal word cards with the objects.

You need

- *Whatever Next!* by Jill Murphy (Macmillan Children's Books)
- A small teddy
- A cardboard box (rocket), colander, Wellington boots, food
- Five separate cards with 1st, 2nd, 3rd, 4th, 5th written on them

Things to ask

Who can remember what Bear found first?

When did Bear look for food?

What object shall we put the '2nd' label next to?

Look, listen, note

Which children can

- say the order in which objects were collected?
- talk about how many objects were put in the rocket?
- match together the label and the object?

Challenge

Children organise a display of the objects and the ordinal labels in the story tent.

Children collect the five objects they would take to the moon.

Words to use

first, second, third, fourth, fifth, last, order, altogether, count, how many?

Maths learning

Number

Using ordinal language

Saying and using number names

Matching ordinal numbers with objects

What's it like?

When reading this story, emphasise the words that describe the little monkey's mother and the word 'not' for what she is *not* like. Discuss with the children how the monkey described his mother and make a list of the words he used. Put out a collection of objects. Children handle them and say what they are like. Describe one with a positive statement: "The object I'm thinking about is wide." Children group together all the possible objects. Say a negative sentence such as: "The object I'm thinking of is not red." Children remove all the objects that are not red. This is more difficult, and the children will need more support. Keep making statements until only one object remains.

You need

- *Monkey Puzzle* by Julia Donaldson and Axel Scheffler (Macmillan Children's Books)
- A collection of everyday objects

Things to ask

Can you say what is the same about these two objects?

How would you describe this pyramid?

Can you tell us how you knew I was thinking of the triangle?

Look, listen, note

Which children can

- describe an object using mathematical words such as 'square', 'heavy' or 'small'?
- indicate two objects that have the same property?
- talk about how to identify a property from a set of objects?

Challenge

Use a Carroll diagram to sort small-world characters into 'is/is not' sets.

Children choose an animal picture and say five 'What it is like' statements and one 'What it is not like' statement.

Words to use

big, bigger, biggest, more, different same, above, small, little, size, shape

Maths learning

Shape and space

Using language to describe the shape and size of objects

Identifying which objects share a particular property

Describing solutions to practical problems

Sleeping

Read the storybook and ask children to give you a 'thumbs up' if they prefer to do any of the activities that Lola does in the book. Instead of going to bed, count together how many children have their thumbs up. Discuss the imaginary animals that appear in the story and suggest making a bucket number line that will help children with counting. Children take a bucket and a label and find that many animals to go in their bucket. They then peg their bucket in the right position on the washing line.

Things to ask

How many dinosaurs do you have in your bucket?

What number label have you attached to your bucket?

What number does your bucket come next on the line?

Look, listen, note

Which children can

- say what the numeral is on their bucket?
- collect the number of animals described on the label?
- decide where on the line to hang their bucket?

Challenge

Children extend the line to 10 buckets.

Children write their own labels.

Working towards the early learning goals in problem solving, reasoning and numeracy

	Art space						Caves and dens						Going to the beach						Market traders						Maths game zone		
	Shape shadows	Texturing	Washing squirts	Cylinder collage	Snail trails	Dry paint	Outdoor den	Superheroes' house	The '10' tent	Wildlife hide	Bear cave	Bookspace	Pebble lines	Collecting shells	Hose patterns	Building up	Rock pools	Fishing	Flower-and-plant stall	Fruit-and-vegetable stall	Baker's stall	Ice-cream stall	Café stall	Seaside stall	Sock it!	Torchlight	Toy track
Say and use number names in order in familiar contexts				●					●		●	●										●			●	●	
Count reliably to 10 everyday objects									●	●	●					●			●	●			●		●	●	●
Recognise numerals 1 to 9									●					●					●								
Begin to use the vocabulary involved in adding and subtracting	●																		●	●	●	●	●	●			●
Use language such as 'more' or 'less' to compare two numbers										●		●		●		●											
Find 'one more' or 'one less' than a number from 1 to 10																											
Begin to relate addition to combining two groups and subtraction to 'taking away'														●					●		●						●
Use language to compare two quantities			●	●				●							●	●						●					
Talk about, recognise and recreate patterns		●	●	●											●												
Use language to describe the shape and size of flat shapes and solids	●	●	●		●	●	●								●	●								●			
Use everyday words to describe position				●							●					●											
Use developing mathematical ideas and methods to solve practical problems	●	●	●	●	●	●	●	●	●	●	●	●	●	●	●	●	●	●	●	●	●	●	●	●	●	●	●

This chart identifies the activities and experiences in *Maths Outside and In* which will support children's developing maths knowledge, skills and understanding so that they can achieve the early learning goals in problem solving, reasoning and numeracy in the Early Years Foundation Stage curriculum.

Workbench								Cooking					Dance studio						'Hands-on' station						Maths workshop						Music studio						Story tent						
Moving gloop	Flying plates	Bunting	Nail number line	Robot builder	Bubbles	Picture frames	Cracker faces	Cookshop	Juicing	Dough play	Choices	Gingerbread men	Follow my leader	Disco dancing	Dancing shoes	Rain dance	Mirror dancing	Dance mats	Cpmpost digging	Exploring tea leaves	A scoop of rice	Play-dough snakes	Papier-mâché modelling	Sticky stufff	Colour move	Our calendar	More or less	I spy numbers	Sort it!	Marbles	Sliding and shaking	Up and down	Outlines	Musical maths box	Sing a song	Nursery rhymes	Jungle animals	Eggs	Rhinoceros	Next thing	What's it like?	Sleeping
			●				●						●	●					●	●					●			●				●										
●	●										●		●						●						●	●	●		●	●		●	●		●			●			●	
			●																								●		●					●							●	
			●						●		●			●						●							●	●	●			●			●	●	●				
										●	●	●															●		●						●	●	●				
											●																●								●	●	●				
													●								●									●					●		●	●				
●	●				●	●		●	●	●										●						●		●			●		●		●			●	●	●		●
							●								●	●	●	●	●			●	●	●										●					●			
	●		●	●	●	●	●		●		●		●		●	●			●		●	●						●							●			●			●	●
●	●	●	●	●	●	●	●	●	●	●	●	●	●	●	●	●	●	●	●	●	●	●	●	●	●	●	●	●	●	●	●	●	●	●	●	●	●	●	●	●	●	●